Library of Congress Cataloging-in-Publication Data

Piers of the California Coast
     by Ed Grant

ISBN 978-0-615-9946-8

Cover Design by Tracey Thomasson

Edited by Mike Wallace and Debra Bronow

Permission to Use from The New York Times, August 6, 2007:
Forward: At Sea Without a Sail by Henry Shukman, page 5

1

TABLE OF CONTENTS

ACKNOWLEDGEMENTS

This book would not have been possible without the help of my extraordinary team of family and friends. My biggest thanks goes to my wife, Barbara and my daughter, Alisha, and my son Daryl, who provided guidance, encouragement and support at all of the crucial points of this journey. The completion of the book was hugely assisted by the enormous effort of the following people who furnished me with guidance and expertise as well as the information that has given this book color and depth: Editors Mike Wallace and Debra Bronow, Serge Dedina, Sylvie Drescher, Christi Forshey, John Fry, Sam George, Trula and Neil Hickman, John Hinkle, Don and Cathy Iglesias, Bruce and Martha Jenkins, Iris King, Larry Kreuger, Molly Lavik, Marikay Lindstrom, Randie Marlow, Frank Quirarte, Sarah Ricker, Stuart Thornton, Tracey Thomasson, Laura Walker, and Grant Washburn.

In addition, a number of people have been enormously helpful and willing and able to contribute their time and effort and provide the perfect advice when I've been in desperate need. This list is includes: Al Arnett, Tim Auringer, Cami Chocarro, Tom Fulton, Cynthia Nelson-Grant, Joel Gringorten, Helen Herrick, Russell Ingrahm, Ward Johnson, Anthony Jufiar, Jim Knier, Nancy Pugh, Bob Schiffner, Stan Smith, Richard Stahler, Lindsay Thomasson, Maddy Wagner.

FORWARD: At Sea Without a Sail

A PIER is a folly, a highway to nowhere. Whether lined with fishermen or filled with the cries and clattering of a roller coaster, whether thick with the aromas of hot dogs and fries or freshly gutted fish, they are there for nothing but the pleasure of humanity. They didn't all begin that way. Piers are not quays or wharves, but many originally were. Most piers in Southern California started life as wharves where steamers could tie up, before the coastal shipping lines were superseded by railroads and highways. Gold in the 1850s, black gold from the 1890s, the silver screen since the 1910s — there has always been a glistening dream to lure people to California, but perhaps none so powerful as the promise of a long pleasure shore, where work is play and enterprise a spiritual adventure. On the day I visited Newport Pier just after Christmas such a fierce wind was blowing that the tide raced under the pier like a fast river. Strollers became staggerers, shielding their eyes from scouring sand. Trash cans gave up their lids to the wind. The whole pier trembled like the sound box of a viola, and mist seethed from the piled up white breakers. On a day like this, what is a pier for? For getting out to sea in a blazing bright storm without ever leaving land. For looking back at the hills and town as you never could from shore. And for feeling O.K. about doing nothing in particular. "Mostly, out on the pier you understand that you're not really on the way to somewhere else. You're already there," is how Jean Femling put it in "Great Piers of California."

A pier is the natural home of courting couples, too, who cavort as the wind whips their hair and coats about, of elderly couples who try to stroll sedately, of families who are out for multigenerational bracing breaths of air and of gulls, which in a wind like this day's, must enjoy the feeling of flying at great speed while hovering motionless above the rails with food.

Part of the charm of these piers comes from the way they thread through the affluence of California with an ordinary workadayness: fishermen pulling up their lines and crab baskets, the Amtrak Pacific Surfliner croaking and clanking by in San Clemente and the rough wooden boards through which you can see the green water stirring in some places. A pod of dolphins might cruise by, a few sea lions might bark hoarsely from the pilings, and a pelican might patrol the long swells. For a moment — far from the suburbia, the freeways, Hollywood and Los Angeles — it might all be a scene from Steinbeck's "Cannery Row." In the mellow air under the creamy sky out over the water, all California seems to be a place of innocence.

by Henry Shukman

Introduction

Photographer and bon vivant Ed Grant grew up combing the beaches of Southern California, embraced by the sands of Newport, Huntington and Long Beach. Like the kernels of silica that became embedded in his toes and other crevices as a lad, Ed could never imagine life without those gateways to the sea — piers. These elevated gangplanks that lead from urban sprawl to the vast unknown, piers give city-dwellers the illusion of control over their manifest destinies.

Ed had an epiphany late one night that these simultaneously hulking and spindly links to our past had never been documented collectively, outside of their respective brochures of 'fun and frolic' in the sun. This book is his love note to the California of his past; land of imagination, perspiration and silicone. It is a tribute to his upbringing, our beach culture and nostalgia for simpler times.

In order to thoroughly document California's piers along the state's entire 770 mile length, Ed Grant spent 4 years photographing 37 of its piers. He chartered a helicopter to first focus in on Los Angeles County piers from a fresh angle, including Malibu and Venice Beach piers. Then he took another spin over San Diego County to cover Oceanside, Imperial Beach, Crystal and Ocean Beach piers by air. Like fingers stretching from their respective communities out into the sea, each pier has a distinct personality of its region. Some like Cayucos Pier in Morro Bay are plain, wooden and utilitarian, while others like Huntington are massive, showy, and sit atop cement and steel pylons — standing vigil over Los Angeles' 3.8 million residents who, like oiled up moths, flock into its arms each summer.

For the past century or so, California's coastal piers have served their masters in a number of disparate ways. From bootlegging to oceanography, billboards to rental cottages, fishing knots to G-string ties, piers have been an integral part of the California lifestyle from the beginning. So, sit back and thumb nostalgically through a few pages of California culture and history though the eyes of its piers. Long may they survive many more El Nino winters with as much character and color as in the past. If not, we shall rebuild them into our own image once again.

— Mike Wallace

"All life is part of a complex relationship in

which each is dependent upon the others;

taking from, giving to and living

with all the rest."

Jacques-Yves Cousteau

Manhattan Beach Pier

by Debra Bronow

It appears out of nowhere. One minute, you're driving west on Manhattan Beach Boulevard, past Polliwog Park and Target. The next minute, you're cresting the hill at Pacific and heading directly for California's oldest standing concrete pier, reaching out toward the horizon with the elegance and dignity you expect from a 97-year-old matriarch. It feels like you are home – along with [35,000] Manhattan Beach residents, and countless visitors from around the world.

For all its iconic beauty, the Manhattan Beach Pier is more than a pretty face. It's the hub of an entire community. At the far end of the pier, there's a tidy little roundhouse with a red tile roof that looks like a relic from another era, when Angelenos rode trolleys to the beach for a day or a week. (In fact, it is fairly new; it was rebuilt in 1992 to look like the original structure, built in 1920 and destroyed by 1988 El Nino storms.) Inside the quaint façade is a bustling marine research lab and teaching aquarium where children come face to face – and sometimes finger to fin – with the same wondrous sea creatures that inhabit the ocean below.

Outside the Roundhouse, families sit together in folding chairs with steaming mugs of coffee and cocoa, waiting patiently for a tug at the fishing lines that stream from the end of the pier down to the ocean. Just past their reach, surfers lounge on their boards, watching for one last perfect wave before they trade their wetsuits in for street clothes and get on with the day.

At the foot of the pier, white sand beaches stretch out in all directions, as clean and inviting as freshly washed linen. It's a great place to take a nap or to pursue a more active agenda. The broad, flat beach has become a favorite place for casual and elite athletes alike. It's home to myriad sporting events: international beach volleyball tournaments such as The Manhattan Beach Open, the Charles Saikley 6-man/6-woman competition, and the International Surf Festival, along with local traditions like the annual Hometown Fair 10K and numerous pier-to-pier events between the Manhattan and Hermosa Beach Piers.

Every summer weekday, colorful easy-ups fill the beach, marking "home base" for the ubiquitous summer camps – beach, surf, junior lifeguards – that have become a bit part of the coming-of-age process for South Bay kids. In December, those same kids are back with their families, turning Manhattan Beach Boulevard into spectator seating for the annual holiday celebration with fireworks launched off the end of the bedecked pier. Each fall, members of local synagogues from the beach cities fill the pier to mark the Jewish New Year by casting their transgressions of the past year – symbolized by bits of bread – into the ocean. (Needless to say, this is a particularly popular event with seagulls and fish!)

One of the greatest local spectacles in Manhattan Beach is the Charlie Saikley 6-Man Volleyball Tournament. Epic volleyball, fun, festivities and beautiful people watching. Saikley was known as the "Godfather of Beach Volleyball," and had run the Manhattan Open since 1965.

Popular beachbreak peaks on either side of the pier. Takes any tide except extreme high. Closes out during large, lined-up swells, so peakier swells are the go, especially SW. An historic seedbed of surf culture, the place where Dale Velzy's first put ten toes over the nose of his surfboard in 1951.

Built in 1920, the 928-foot Manhattan Beach Pier is California's oldest standing concrete pier. Its circular shape was designed by engineer A. L. Harris to deflect the impact of waves and wind.

Manhattan Beach Pier

The Roundhouse Marine Lab and Aquarium at the end of the pier is a research and teaching facility that introduces thousands of children to marine biology each year.

Manhattan Beach Pier

Santa Monica Pier

by Debra Bronow

The story of the Santa Monica Pier follows the same scrappy, boom-and-bust (and boom-again) plot line that characterizes Los Angeles and California history. It's a story that starts with the most basic of our human functions, but it goes on to reveal our greatest complexities: the hopes and dreams, the false starts and fresh beginnings, the intersection of imagination and commerce, our yearning for adventure and our attempts to strike a balance between the natural world and creature comforts. This is where cross-country journeys on Route 66 – and later, the Interstate 10 freeway – ended, where movies were made, romances were kindled, and Popeye was born. Many of California's piers took shape at the turn of the 20th century, and most were meant to connect people to the sea. They were hubs of the community; they accommodated recreational and commercial fishing, a growing shipping industry, or they offered a year-round version of the boardwalks, vacation homes, and amusements that attracted tourists and recent transplants from the East Coast.

The Santa Monica Pier, on the other hand, was built to meet a less attractive, but far more urgent need for the city's burgeoning population: sewage disposal. The 1600-foot pier was built to support – and disguise – a pipe that carried treated sewage into the ocean (a practice that ended just a few years later). When construction was completed in 1909, the opening day festivities focused not on its function as part of a public utility, but on its state-of-the art engineering as the first all-concrete pier on the west coast. The day-long dedication was filled with athletic events, a visit from the USS Albany, and celebrity surfer George Freeth. At sunset, the celebration drew to a close with "The Surrender of Rex Neptune," a tableau vivant performance in which Rex Neptune, king of the sea, promised that the new pier would meet the same fate as so many wooden piers that he regularly destroyed. When Queen Santa Monica pointed out that the pier was made of solid concrete, Neptune took a spectacular, flame-engulfed dive back into the ocean. (Just ten years later, the "indestructible" concrete pier nearly collapsed due to rust damage; it was shored up with creosote-treated wood pilings.)

In spite of what ran through the pipes underneath the deck, public transportation and its bountiful supply of sea life – everything from anchovies to giant black sea bass – made the Santa Monica pier immediately popular as a fishing spot. Its potential was also evident to entrepreneur Charles Looff, who got his start carving carousel horses and went on to develop and run amusement parks. The fact that the original municipal pier was too narrow for an amusement park didn't stop Looff: he built an adjacent, wider pier just to its south.

By 1916, the Looff Hippodrome opened with a carousel, the first attraction of the new Looff Pleasure Pier. The same year, the US Congress considered legislation to designate public highways, promising an interstate route connecting Chicago to Los Angeles, and Looff expanded the pier's offerings to include a roller coaster, bowling alley, fun house, live music and picnic area in anticipation of a boom in population, tourism, and the growing entertainment industry.

By 1924, the California Dream was in full swing. The burgeoning economy was matched by endless sunshine and optimism. A breakwater and yacht harbor opened that year, bringing recreational sailing and paddleboarding to the harbor. The Santa Monica Amusement company acquired the Looff Pleasure Pier and upgraded the old Big Streak roller coaster with the bigger, faster Whirlwind Dipper. They also started work on a 15,000 square-foot ballroom, billed as the largest in the world at the time. In 1926, the La Monica Ballroom opened, and the "floating castle over the water" was immediately the most popular night spot in town – to the point that it caused Santa Monica's first traffic jam on opening night.

The Great Depression, of course, changed everything. Tourists on Route 66 were largely replaced by desperate refugees from the dust bowl, and they weren't making their way to California to dance. By the mid 1930s, the huge ballroom was repurposed, first as a convention center, then as lifeguard headquarters, and for a short time it housed the city jail. In spite of the hard times, the pier continued to attract visitors – and some creative "business" schemes, including an offshore gambling boat that used the pier as the launch for a water taxi service until federal officials shut it down in a spectacular 8-day stand-off, complete with water hoses and a mobster in need of a haircut. During World War II, when other major piers were used for Naval operations, Santa Monica became a major commercial fishing port.

By the end of the war, things were looking up again. The Hippodrome had a new carousel, and music filled the La Monica ballroom again. By the 1960s, age had taken its toll on the breakwater, the municipal pier and its sidekick, but no viable plans for its restoration were emerging. In 1973, Santa Monica's city manager proposed that the pier be demolished and replaced with a new bridge to a man-made island. The community came out in droves to protect the pier's historic status, but it continued to languish for ten years, until heavy storms forced a major renovation. At the same time, Heal the Bay and other organizations began efforts to restore the increasingly polluted water and coastline.

Today, the pier is refreshed and revived. It features many of the same attractions – albeit updated – as it did in its youth. A nine-story Ferris wheel glitters at the end, next to a roller coaster, a fun zone, and other rides. Live music rings out over the water again; the city hosts a series of free outdoor concerts on the pier every summer. Cirque du Soleil tents rise up from the parking lot on a regular basis. Luxury hotels are strategically located within walking and viewing distance of the landmark. And of course, the fishing is still pretty good.

The Santa Monica Yacht Harbor sign has been welcoming visitors ince 1941, it's iconic mid-centrury design is a reminder of the Pier's long history.

Proof that there's more to the Santa Monica Pier than just the Pacific Park fun zone!

Newer, bigger, and wilder than the original, the Santa Monica Pier roller coaster is a thrilling tribute to Blue Streak Racer, which opened on what was then the Loof Pleasure Pier in 1917.

Santa Monica Pier

In spite of the many activities and attractions on the deck of the Santa Monica Pier, it is still, after all, a connection between land and the sea.

The physics of flying are demonstrated - and taught - daily at the Trapeze School of New York's west coast campus.

Santa Monica Pier

For weary cross-country travelers, the Santa Monica Pier was more than the end of the road — it was a symbol of having arrived with countless hopes and dreams.

Malibu Pier

by John Hinkle

Quite possibly the most photographed pier on the California coast, the Malibu Pier has served as a backdrop for golden age Hollywood movies, the Gidget and Beach Blanket Bingo "surfing" movies, high fashion photo shoots and over 75 surf movies. Most often, however, it will be seen as framing countless iconic surfing images that include the legends Bob Simmons, Matt Kivlin and Dave Sweet of the 1930's-40's to Lance Carson, Miki Dora, Dewey Weber, Butch Linden and Johnny Fain in the 1950's-60's, and so on through the 70's, 80's, and 90's of J. Riddle, Allan Sarlo and Josh Farberow. Today, Dane Peterson, Kassia Meador and the Marshall Brothers are found gracing the silhouette of the Mailbu Pier.

On big south swells at Surfrider Beach, the perfect wave ratchets, reels and races deep off First Point, across the bay and lines up on through the pier. Only locals like Sarlo brave shooting the pier. Tragically on June 9, 1951, Nick Gabaldon, the coast's earliest known African American surfer, died after hitting the pier on a solid eight foot swell.

On flat summer days, the bored groms will either paddle race to the end of the pier and back or perhaps dare each other to jump off the end of it and swim to shore. Through the 20th century and still to this day, the Malibu Pier serves as a bookend to the classic waves of First Point and a landmark as the heart of Malibu and as surf culture mecca.

The Malibu Pier was originally built in 1905 for Frederick Hastings Rindge's Malibu Rancho, to transfer agricultural products, goods and materials to and from vessels. The Adamson House, located just west of the pier, includes a wall that lined the highway to the pier built in 1932. The pier entrance tower and wall is decorated with Malibu Potteries tile from that era and remains today. The pier was opened to the public in 1934 and during World War II, the end of the pier served as a U.S. Coast Guard daylight lookout station.

Long time residents remember spending many hours in 1972 into the 90's at Alice's Restaurant (named for Arlo Guthrie's song). Throughout the years, Malibu Pier suffered heavy damage from El Nino storms of 1993 and 1995 and was declared unsafe and closed to the public in 1995. After restoring the pier to it's 1950's historic look, it was reopened to the public in 2008 and is now owned by California Parks and Recreation.

Every September, the Malibu Surfing Association hosts the Malibu Surfing Association Classic Invitational and surfers from Hawaii, Australia, Japan, Taiwan, Mexico, Spain, France,

Virginia Beach and Californians from San Diego to Santa Cruz come to participate and compete in the historically perfect waves of Malibu. The MSA often held fundraisers on

the pier during the event, screening surf movies, displaying classic Woodie wagons or catering for the contestants. All traveling surfers know they've made it to the world famous beach by recognizing the perfect waves off First Point to the West and the famed Malibu Pier to the East. It truly is a gem, a treasure within the shadow of Los Angeles.

On October 9, 2010, this stretch of beach from the Malibu Colony to the Malibu Pier was enshrined as the first World Surfing Reserve. The designation establishes the unique value of the Malibu coastal environment and aims to enhance efforts to maintain the pristine nature of the area.

The Malibu Pier has served as a backdrop for the golden age of Hollywood movies and for such films as Gidget and Beach Blanket Bingo. There have been over 75 surf movies filmed here as well as countless photo shoots.

Malibu Pier

Venice Pier

by Christie Forshey

Venice is an eccentric, artsy, diverse community pumping with businesses, residents and tourists. Founded in 1905 as a seaside resort town by developer Abbot Kinney, Venice is known like its' namesake in Italy for its' canals. Combined with fabulous beaches and a "circus-like" ocean front, street performers, Muscle Beach and streetballers play and fill the environment with daily amusement. The piers in Venice show a history of destruction, affluence, neglect and rebirth. The first Abbot Kinney Venice pier was never even used because 1905 winter storms destroyed it. Thousands of workers labored to rebuild in time for 4th of July with 1200 feet extending into the Pacific Ocean. By 1910, the pier included amusements including an Aquarium, Virginia Reel, Whip, Racing Derby, bowling alley and game booths. In December of 1920, the Kinney Pier was destroyed by fire.

The Kinney family rebuilt quickly to compete with neighboring amusement piers. Larger than ever with three roller coasters, Fun House and Flying Circus aerial ride with hired aviators to do aerial stunts over the beach...it was named the finest amusement pier on the West Coast. A hundred thousand tourists visited on weekends. In 1924, another fire destroyed the entire pier.

Several political situations changed Venice. Annexation from Los Angeles (1930s), the Great Depression, Prohibition and even World War II impacted the waterfront with evening curfews and National Guardsmen patrolling beaches for enemy ships. In 1946, Los Angeles City ordered the Kinney Company's Venice Pier to be closed and demolished. Neglect followed and by the 50s, Venice was named the "Slum by the Sea".

In the 60s gang activity and beat Generation, 70s art revival, and 80s and 90s street performers and bands have shaped the Venice that is the eccentric, artsy and diverse area known today.

The current Venice Pier at the end of Washington Boulevard opened in 1964 extends a quarter mile into the Pacific Ocean. It too has faced storms and destruction which once closed the pier for a decade. With its' last repair in 2006, is a simple concrete structure with a 120-foot diameter circular end. The Venice Pier is a free fishing pier and visitors walk its length for the beauty and unobstructed view.

Venice Pier is no longer a pier of amusements, but a pier of simple pleasures, 1310 feet long and one-half mile from the famous Venice Boardwalk, which has plenty of amusements.

Venice Pier

Hermosa Beach Pier

by Debra Bronow

Hermosa – Spanish for "beautiful" – is an apt name for this cozy little beach city, with 20 parks, a lush greenbelt, and two linear miles of white sand shoreline within its 1.43 square-mile footprint. The Hermosa Beach Pier, too, lives up to its name, with the kind of beauty that requires no embellishments: simple and elegant, it reaches nearly a quarter-mile into the waves.

On a clear day, it's possible to stand at the end of the pier and take in the expanse of the entire Santa Monica Bay, framed by the Santa Monica Mountains to the north and the cliffs of Palos Verdes to the south, and Catalina Island perched far out on the horizon in between them. It's a vantage point that affords a good chance of spotting a pod of dolphins playing in the waves, or even – at the right time of year and with a decent set of binoculars – migrating gray whales, fin whales, and Orcas.

Looking towards the shore, the hills of Hermosa Beach are a charming, colorful mix of vintage beach bungalows and sleek new homes; farther still are the foothills and mountains that surround the Los Angeles basin.

Breathtaking as they are, there is more to the Hermosa Beach pier than its views. To walk its length is to be immersed in a world uncluttered by time or commerce. There is just the concrete under your feet, with its tiny cracks and fractures telling stories about standing up to countless winter storms. There is the simple steel guardrail, topped by wooden handrails that have weathered to the same silver-gray as the inviting benches that line both sides of the pier, offering a comfortable seat for quiet contemplation, a little fishing, or a perfect view of the action in the water and on the beach. Midway, a Surfer's Hall of Fame acknowledges the important heritage of the sport in Hermosa Beach along with legends of the sport. Each year, new members are inducted, adding to the row of brass plaques embedded in the concrete pathway.

In many ways, the City of Hermosa Beach was built around its pier. A wooden pier was first built by the Hermosa Land and Water Company in 1904, two years before the city was incorporated. Destroyed by a storm in 1913, it was replaced the next year with a concrete pier. By 1965, the original concrete pier met the fate of its predecessor, and a new concrete pier was built in its place. Over the years, it has been buffeted and damaged by storms, and occasionally closed for repairs, but it remains a beloved focal point for the community. Years ago, buildings at the base of the pier housed not only lifeguards, but the Hermosa Beach Public Library and a performing arts theater.

In truth, the pier experience extends far beyond the LA County Southern lifeguard headquarters, Schumacher Plaza and the sculpture of surfing pioneer Tim Kelly at its base. It really starts at the intersection of Pier and Hermosa Avenues, where the antique green clock tower marks the spot where cars stop and the walking starts. As with the pier itself, it's easy to get lost in time on the Pier Avenue Pedestrian Plaza; some of Hermosa Beach's long-time favorite restaurants and clubs co-exist with newer establishments. Vintage clothing shops, a high-end tattoo artist, surf shops and fashion boutiques are all tucked in together. Pier Avenue and the pier are the the backdrop for myriad annual events: summer concerts, Fiesta Hermosa, the International Surf Festival, and countless pier-to-pier runs, walks, and swims. 71 volleyball courts line the beach on the north and south sides of the pier, and the water is almost always peppered with people and boards - surf, body, and paddle. Friendly, eclectic, and welcoming, the Hermosa Beach Pier is an easy place to spend the day.

Though the headquarters for the LA County Lifeguards Southern Section looks like a traditional beach cottage with its wooden decks and whitewashed railings, this thoroughly state-of-the-art building was dedicated in 2005 as part of a pier modernization project.

A bronze statue of surf and lifeguard legend, Tim Kelly, commemorates his legacy and the history of surfing in Hermosa Beach.

Hermosa Beach Pier

Pier Avenue, the entrance to the pier and one of the beach community's main shopping, eating and partying areas.

Strong and relentless, the wind and waves of the Pacific have taken their toll on the Hermosa Beach pier over the years. Built and rebuilt three times since 1904, repaired countless times and modernized again in 2005, the pier remains a stoic, beloved landmark in the South Bay.

Hermosa Beach Pier

Hermosa Beach Pier

Redondo Beach Pier

by Christi Forshey

The Redondo Beach Pier is the largest "Endless Pier" on the California coastline. It has an irregular shape, also known as the Horseshoe Pier and from North to South includes King Harbor, the International Boardwalk, Fisherman's Wharf and Veteran's Park, which houses the historic Redondo Library. The pier is a gathering place for families, tourists, fisherman and locals. Originally a tourist attraction in the 1900s, rail lines ran along the shore and to the end of the pier as lumber started to arrive from the Northwest. Soon visitors walked out to the end of the pier awaiting passenger ships. From 1910-1920s, Redondo Pier was one of the best-attended weekend getaway spots in America. At that time, the Lighting Racer Roller Coaster was located on the sand and the Hotel Redondo, Pavilion Casino and Bath House (claimed to be the largest salt water plunge in the world) drew booming crowds. When Prohibition began, the casino closed which soon affected Hotel Redondo livelihood.

In its' current Horseshoe formation, which was rebuilt with wooden pilings in 1929, the pier incorporates design elements of the 1916 concrete Horseshoe that was destroyed by a fierce winter storm in 1919. Parts of the wooden structure exist today, however, in 1988, one third of the wooden pier was destroyed by fire. A Channel 4 YouTube clip from May 1988, explains that the chemically treated wooden pier lit up like a torch due to an electrical short under the Breaker's Restaurant. In 1995, after much public debate, the pier was reconstructed to connect remaining wooded structures with new construction.

Today, old and new merchants coexist and draw diverse crowds. Crab markets, Naja's Place with live music and 88 beers on tap; Old Tony's where you can watch the sunset in the Crow's Nest, purchase Mai Tai's and keep the glass; eat at Hotdog on A Stick or visit the Fun Factory, a retro arcade; which all draw loyal consumers and tourists. Fishermen line the edges of the pier daily and pull their catch from 25 feet below. Stand up paddleboard lessons, fishing expeditions, gondola rides and whale watch excursions are all available here!

Since Redondo Beach became a city in 1892, Redondo has seen seven different piers. Revitalization of the pier has been constant and controversial amongst residents. Current renovation plans are in the works to rejuvenate fifteen acres of pier and harbor land. Boutique hotels, chain stores and high rises want to move in.

Rich with history and culture, Redondo Pier is ever changing. The railroad lines, casino, bathhouse and Hotel Redondo are now history. Come today to explore King Harbor, the International Boardwalk, Fisherman's Wharf and Veteran's Park. Redondo hosts an annual Kite Festival, Summer concert series, weekly Farmer's Market and Lobster Festival. Walk the Redondo Beach Pier and storefronts before large surf or builders change it again... Like the Redondo Pier's nickname, the possibilities are "Endless!"

Strolling above the Pacific Ocean or taking a boat ride, the Redondo Beach Pier has an abundance of activities. The Pier offers boating, swimming, fishing, shopping, biking and in-line skating or you can relax in the parks and listen to live music.

Redondo Beach Pier

Belmont Veterans Memorial Pier

by Larry Krueger

Born of the tensions on land, built in the storms of the sea, the Belmont Veterans Memorial Pier is a landmark in Long Beach life and activities. In 1908, residents of the Belmont Heights community, in the city Long Beach, asked the city to build them a pier. After being denied and tired of paying high taxes, the residents broke from the City of Long Beach and formed the city of Belmont Heights. But after just one year, the determination to build the new pier failed. The residents returned to the City of Long Beach who had now promised to build them a new pier. In 1911, the construction of the new pier began. On Christmas Eve 1915, thousands came for the opening of the new 975 foot wooden pier. The official name was the Grand Avenue Pier, but Belmont Heights residents called it the Belmont Heights Pier and many locals called it the Devils Gate Pier due to the natural rock formation nearby. The original wooden pier stood for over 50 years, but the relentless sea finally took toll and a new pier needed to be built.

In 1966, a new 1620 foot concrete pier was begun and in 1967, the pier officially had it's grand opening. Located just south of the original wooden pier, the official name was the Belmont Veterans Memorial Pier in honor of United States veterans.

Today, the pier is the hub of aquatic life and the center of recreational activity. Located next to the pier is the Belmont Olympic Plaza Pool. Housed in a Greco-Modern building five stories high, this pool has been the competing and training place of Olympians Mark Spitz and Michael Phelps. The beach surrounding the pier has a beautiful bike and running path, as well as, over 30 beach volleyball courts where Olympian Misty May has trained and held clinics. Due to the pier's location in the San Pedro Bay, strong predominant northwesterly winds blow in the afternoon and the ocean around the pier becomes alive with kite surfers and sailboats. On any given afternoon over 50 kites can be seen with surfers racing near the pier and jumping waves. The Congressional Cup of sailing is held here and sailors from all around the world compete, coming within inches of the pier as they seek to win the cup for their nation.

All year the pier is central to activities and events. Restaurants sit at the base of the pier where people can enjoy a meal and drink. "Bouys" is the restaurant located at the end of the pier where people can dine and look out over the ocean. The daily afternoons see families and couples enjoying sunsets overlooking the Queen Mary and downtown Long Beach where the Grand Prix is raced in April. In the summer months, events include fishing rodeos for kids, Pirate Day Invasions, and a 4th of July party overlooking the fireworks from the Queen Mary. For people visiting by water, the pier has an Aqualink that can take visitor to downtown areas, as well as, south toward Seal Beach. The Belmont Veterans Memorial Pier is central to recreational sports and activities in the city of Long Beach, hence Long Beach is known as the, "Aquatics Capital of America."

Compared with other area piers , Long Beach's is not quite as picturesque. Looking out you see cargo ships, oil tankers, artificial oil drilling islands and, most prominently, the cranes of the Port of Long Beach. But it's location is unique among piers on the Southern California coast because of the protection from the surge and surf of the Pacific Ocean. There is the breakwater, a 2.5-mile rock wall 1.5 miles off the city's coast that benefits boaters and offers protection from ocean swells. Also, the offshore waters are famous for the Congressional Cup, one of the major international sailing events. The one-on-one format is the same as the America's Cup and many of the winners of the Congressional Cup have gone on to compete in the America's Cup.

SEAL BEACH POLICE DEPARTMENT
THE DICK HALEY COMMUNITY SAFETY BUILDING EST.1995

Seal Beach Pier

Seal Beach Pier

by Larry Krueger

The city of Seal Beach was recently listed as number four in a recent Forbes Magazines Friendliest Cities in America. Central to its warm friendly environment is the Seal Beach Pier. Nestled between the San Gabriel River to the west and Anaheim Bay to the east, the Seal Beach Pier has a rich history.

First known as Bay City, the original founding father of Seal Beach was Phillip Stanton. Stanton sold the first piece of property to John Ord who became the first resident of Bay City. Stanton then formed the Bayside Land Co. and began to sell subdivisions. Soon the electric Red Cars came to Bay City with potential real estate developers and the town began to grow. In 1906, the first pier was built to attract tourists and because of the confusion with San Francisco and the playful seals on the beach, on October 27, 1915 Bay City became Seal Beach.

In 1916 a new pier was built for what would become known as the Joy Zone. At the end of the new pier were 50 enormous scintillator lights, which could be seen for twenty miles and on the weekends fireworks were set off to entertain tourists. Finally, a rollercoaster

called the "Derby" was imported from San Francisco and the Joy Zone was complete and became the first Disneyland of Southern California.

During this time many silent movies were filmed in Seal Beach including Cecil B. Demille's "The Ten Commandments" parting of the Red Sea scene. Two pavilions were built at the entrance to the pier, the Jewel Café and the Bathhouse with a plunge and a moving dance floor upstairs. The Seal Beach pier had arrived.

In 1929, the Great Depression brought an end to the Joy Zone and a fire burned down the "Derby" rollercoaster. During this time, Seal Beach became known as "Sin City." Prohibition brought Casinos for gambling, hotels for prostitution, and rum running to Seal Beach due to a lack of police enforcement. In 1939, a hurricane in the south Pacific ripped the Seal Beach Pier in half. Shortly after, the pier was rebuilt and World War II began.

During the War years, the pier was primarily used for military purposes and slowly Seal Beach reestablished conservative roots. People began to move to Seal Beach to raise families. When the war ended in 1945 the City of Seal Beach put the pier up for lease and on January 1, 1946. Art Lescher and Myrle Stockton took over the pier and ran the operations from 1945–1961. This was the birth of a new era for the Seal Beach Pier.

Lescher and Stockton brought 3 sport fishing boats from Huntington Beach, the Seal Beach Café was opened at the end of the pier and a tram was purchased to take people and their fishing gear to the end of the pier. The Seal Beach Pier was back in action. The small town community now attracted fisherman from all around to catch halibut, yellowtail, albacore, barracuda, and a variety of other fish species.

Unfortunately, in 1983 a giant northwest swell once again destroyed 120 feet of the pier. But like a Phoenix, the pier would rise again. With the help of the local residents the pier was restored. A wooden pier was built making it the second longest wooden pier in California and keeping the old rustic look.

Today, the Seal Beach pier is still the center of attraction for locals and tourists alike. When you walk onto the Seal Beach pier you are met by "Slick" the seal. At sunrise the activities start. Old men gather with their coffees to talk about days gone by. Surfers check the surf before paddling out and fisherman eagerly walk to the end of the pier in hopes of a prize catch. As the morning arrives, parents bring children to the small playground next to the pier and runners exercise a long the beach. On each side of the pier is Eisenhower Park where art festivals take place and in the summer months concerts in the park. At the beach around the pier rough water swimming events take place, as well as, kite festivals and sand castle building contests. Surfers enjoy the peaks on the southside and the long lefts on the northside of the pier. In the evenings, after dining at one of the pubs or restaurants on Main Street, families and lovers come to watch the picturesque sunsets over Catalina Island. The Seal Beach pier continues to be a jewel on the California coast. Perhaps this is why Seal Beach is often called, "Mayberry by the sea."

Photo Courtesy of Larry Krueger

Seal Beach Lifeguard Department operates year round to protect beachgoers along the city's two-mile stretch of beach and surfside.

Super Moon and reflections of Seal Beach Pier at sunset.

Seal Beach Pier

Huntington Beach Pier

by Mike Wallace

The City of Huntington lies approximately 39 miles southeast of LAX at a dead trot across the Palos Verdes Peninsula. To the west are the nearest Channel Islands of Santa Catalina, San Clemente and San Nicolas. To the east is Anaheim, where Mickey found stardom, and Santa Ana, from whence the offshore winds blow. To the immediate south are Newport Beach, Dana Point and San Clemente, all sparkling beach towns in their own right.

Huntington Pier is a product of its environment. The pier was rebuilt at least four times, in 1912, 1939, 1983 and 1988. Last fully rebuilt in 1992, it is a fortress of cement and steel, punctuated by Ruby's Diner at the tip of its 1,856-feet in length. It is not the longest pier along the California coast, a title which belongs to the Santa Cruz Wharf at 2,745-feet, but it is one of the more imposing structures. On the National Register of Historic Places, the pier was redesigned by Moffat and Nichol Engineers to withstand both huge 30-foot swells and violent earthquakes.

The pier has three hexagonal platforms spaced along its length with a final massive diamond-shaped platform on which red-roofed Ruby's is built with 360 degree views of the coast. The Pier Plaza at the other end houses an open-air amphitheater for concerts at its base and there's even a weekly farmer's market. Named after surfing's founding father, Duke's restaurant serves more upscale Cali-Hawaiian fare. Wide bike paths, ample parking, camping, beach volleyball courts and fire pits are also Huntington features.

The iconic pier is a hub of Southern California beach culture and symbolic through its past incarnations of the Huntington community's ability to continually reinvent itself. In its natural state the region was a swampy marshland, inhabited by the Gabrielino-Tongva Indians who roamed the Los Angeles Basin, fishing and subsisting along the shifting Los Angeles, San Gabriel and Santa Ana Rivers. European settlers soon arrived with the Spanish missions and military. Soldier Manuel Nieto was deeded the first large parcel of land in the area, which became known as Rancho Los Nietos. In fact, Beach Boulevard which stretches a few miles from the 405 Freeway to the Pacific

Coast Highway was originally the route for cattle drives from inland to the city center.

Tourism was an early part of the Huntington economy, as Henry Huntington acquired the rights to develop the region via his Huntington Beach Company by leveraging his extension of the railroad to the area. Surrounding lands that weren't under development or under wetlands were primarily agricultural, sowing sugar beets and the like. The city that bears his name was incorporated on February 17, 1909. And Henry had a knack for commerce and promoting his investments.

Then came the oil boom, which littered the region with wells and pumps that still rhythmically rise and nod in the scrubby remaining undeveloped flats that pock the region. From that gritty and industrial beginning the City of Huntington sprawled toward the coast and reclaimed valuable beachfront property for condos, hotels, restaurants and businesses that make it the surf tourism Mecca that it is today. Jan and Dean's 1963 chart topper "Surf City" was reputed to anoint Huntington with that title, which they legally wrested from Santa Cruz in the courts nearly 30-year later after the two cities battled for the exclusive rights to that crown. In 2008, Huntington settled its lawsuit with a Santa Cruz T-shirt vendor for use of that slogan, which has subsequently been franchised and used to aid local businesses.

Huntington typically hosts as many as 50 amateur and professional surf competitions per year culminating with the massive annual week-long surf festival on the south side of the pier – the US Open of Surfing. Starting back in 1959 with the West Coast Surfing Championships, this annual event has gone through many incarnations, becoming the U.S. Surfing Championships in 1964, then the OP Pro in 1982 before finally becoming the U.S. Open of Surfing in 1994. Several different sponsors have stepped up to run the event, most recently Vans US Open of Surfing, which can draw as many as half a million visitors who drop over $21 million into the local economy. The Open typically houses an array of extreme sports events and related vendors, including a "Coastal Carnage" and "Damn Am" skateboard competitions (bowl- and street-style), sponsors beach stores, plus two stages for bands to keep the writhing masses entertained between surf heats. The Open is considered the largest surf-themed event in the world.

The "Surfing Walk of Fame" and "Surfers' Hall of Fame" add members in ceremonies during the Open. Selected by a swathe of surf industry tycoons, categories include Surfing Champion, Woman of the Year, Local Hero, Surf Pioneer, Surf Culture and Honor Roll for the Walk of Fame, which imbeds granite plaques in the sidewalks across from the Pier at the corner of Main and PCH.

Open ocean swells from both the northern and southern hemispheres wrap around the Channel Islands, which diffuse and diffract these swells before they meet the sand banks built up around the pier, creating rideable peaks almost year-round. Surfers who have mastered the waves south of the pier know how to link the abrupt "pier bowl" on the outside or "Machado left" (named after soul-surfer Rob Machado) with stylish turns through the soft mid-section to the inside runners, which jack up again and offer room for a couple quick hits before the wave expires on the sand at the feet of cheering throngs. Some intrepid (or foolhardy) surfers are known on occasion to "shoot the pier," angling through mussel-encrusted pilings to blow out the north-side to impress the judges and startle beach bathers. On smaller days competitors will paddle right out under the pier between the two rows of pilings, propelled by the rip and using this modest cover from cresting waves.

Like Los Angeles, Huntington Pier is all about marketing the lifestyle, living the dream, SoCal swagger. Hollister, the California-themed clothing chain, has even gone so far as to pipe in streaming video of surf from the pier into all their stores, for which they pay the city a fee that goes toward water safety equipment for local lifeguards.

Go for it !!!

This is a good one. It's one of the best waves of the morning, and I am going to shoot the pier!

Got it. Whoa, late drop. Don't eat it! Get the nose up. Center balance and redirect the speed. Sweet!

Should I? It's coming up fast. I am going to do it. Go for the first gap. The gap before the piling with the big chunk out of it... or maybe the slot right behind it? One of them will be good.

This is a nice section, with lots of push. I'm screaming along, and I can feel the long period in the swell.

What if I don't make it? That piling is probably covered with barnacles. The wave I have chosen is not too big. This is Huntington, not Maverick's... but even a small one will smash a surfer into a piling if the timing is wrong. Or if that cross chop trips him up.

Pull out! I shouldn't be trying this at all. I'm being Stupid! Why even tempt fate? I'm going to get raked over this giant cheese grater, and probably split my melon. SPLAT! Imagine the wounds this is going to inflict! Huge gouges... like being shredded by a polar bear or clubbed by a redwood.

I wonder if anyone has ever bled to death after colliding with this pier?

It's too late to pull out. The current is stronger here, sucking right into the pilings. I am already too close! My wave has doubled up, and it is not going to let me off. This stupid thing WANTS to sweep me into the massive bear claws and the claws are getting closer, and bigger, and they are welcoming the encounter. They are like huge teeth, and the pier is hungry.

This was a bad decision.

Well, I asked for it. I had been purposely edging toward it all session, knowing I wanted to challenge the towering obstacle. Surfers had been shooting the Huntington Beach Pier since the dawn of the sport.

I was channeling Greg Noll! Seizing the moment, fearlessly committing to the section, and taking dead aim at the gap by the piling with the chunk. Or the gap behind it. But now I was missing those gaps.

If I kick off now I'll be right in there, and probably get smashed into the barnacles for trying to escape. I like this board, and now it's going to get splintered on this dumb pier. I'm going to be ground into hamburger, or splattered into the thick trunk of a tar covered post.

Watch that cross wedge! Don't fall here!

I have to go for it. Any other decision will be a mistake at this stage. Like a skydiver, I am committed. I jumped out of the plane and I can't go back.

I'm going to shoot it.

What a rush!

On most days, the surf at the pier is nothing out of the ordinary, especially if you are not interested in being part of the dawn patrol. However, on those occasions when a storm rolls in, or a swell rolls in from points far out in the Pacific, large waves can be seen crashing in to the pier and that is when things get interesting.

Bruce Brown –

Huntington Beach and its pier have been iconic locations for numerous films and television shows. On this occasion, Fuel TV dedicates a special program to Bruce Brown, honoring him for his ground-breaking surfing documentaries, the crown jewel of which is enshrined as 'The Endless Summer.' He had made four feature-length films prior to making this one, but this film's incredible cult and mainstream success made him the father of California surf culture. Undoubtedly the best-known surfing documentary ever made, the premise was simple; take two surfers 'round the globe and create a perfect escapist parable – an endless Summer of sun, surf, and girls (but mostly surf).

From the West Coast of Africa to South Africa, Australia, islands of the Pacific and Hawaii we go. Swept along with two young men from California, we witness them introduce the sport of surfing to people who have never seen a surfboard before. Hilarity ensues as villagers in Ghana and Senegal try to surf a longboard in heavy surf for the first time, and Bruce's pitch-perfect narration accompanies relaxing sounds of the surf guitar. Of course it helps to include Mike Hynson and Robert August, among the best young surfers of their time,

style masters on uncharted waves. In an innocent age before the beaches got jammed with jet skis, racing boats, and of course more surfers, Endless Summer is a time capsule, just as entertaining now as it was when it was first released.

John Van Hamersveld designed the iconic movie poster, using a photograph shot at Salt Creek Beach in Dana Point. He positioned Bruce Brown in the foreground, surfboard on head. Between him and the oversized sun stand the film's two stars: Mike Hynson and Robert August. Van Hamersveld He turned a photo into an abstract design by reducing each color to a single tone, taking a negative and making it a positive, then silk-screening the result. And he did all this at his kitchen table in Dana Point, slicing the photo to bring its three surfers closer together, using Day-Glo paint and hand-lettering "The Endless Summer" at the bottom. "He quantified the entire surf culture in that one image," says Dave Tourje, a colleague and director of the Chouinard School of Art in L.A. "The movie's great but I believe the image is more powerful and more enduring than the movie itself."

The Endless Summer

On any day of the year it's summer somewhere in the world. Bruce Brown's latest color film highlights the adventures of two young American surfers, Robert August and Mike Hynson who follow this everlasting summer a-round the world. Their unique expedition takes them to Senegal, Ghana, Nigeria, South Africa, Australia, New Zealand, Tahiti, Hawaii and California. Share their experiences as they search the world for that perfect wave which may be forming just over the next Horizon. **BRUCE BROWN FILMS**

Newport Pier

by Debra Branow

For the better part of my life, I've lived a stone's throw from some of the Pacific's most breathtaking coastlines. As a child in American Samoa, we learned which beaches were safe for swimming, which ones required shoes, which ones were favorites for catching Octopus by hand, and which were off limits entirely. On Wake Island, we dared one another to go into the concrete WWII bunkers along the shoreline; though we weren't particularly frightened by the idea that the squat buildings could be haunted by any number of unfortunate soldiers, we were put off by the smell of countless sea creatures that seemed to have died there. Our government-issue house was separated from the vast North Pacific Ocean by two gravel berms that seemed pointless until typhoon season, when giant waves jumped effortlessly over the berms and up to our doorsteps. Later, we whistled our way through winters in Northwestern Alaska, making the Northern Lights dance above the ice for us; and when the ice began to come and go with the tides of the Chukchi and Bering Seas, we knew that we would soon see racks of ruby-colored salmon drying along the beach. My own kids were born and raised in Manhattan Beach, and they measured seasons by the local pier: beach camp drop-off in the summer, hot cocoa and fireworks in the winter; Fiesta Hermosa on Memorial Day and Labor Day weekends.

For all the oceanic variety in my life, if the word "beach" or "pier" is mentioned in conversation, it is always the Newport Beach Pier that comes to mind, bringing with it a flood of sense memories. My father's job with the FAA made for a peripatetic life, and we returned home to Southern California once a year at best. As kids, my siblings and I knew that our rare visits had two sure bets: time with grandparents in La Verne and a stay in Newport Beach. We came to think of the little weekly rental cottage on 27th and Balboa as "ours," because we returned year after year.

It was a perfect location, and it shaped our daily rituals: mornings on the beach for kids, fishing off of the pier for dad, then a meet-up on the pier later in the day. Even now, the smell of Coppertone, salt air and seaweed calls to those perfect summer days: the hot cement of the Boardwalk, the tickle of a sand crab in my palm, the thrill of dodging and diving through the waves – or getting swirled and tossed, landing back on shore with a bathing suit full of sand once we were deemed old enough (and brave enough) to body surf.

The Balboa Peninsula has changed considerably since those days, but much of it is surprisingly the same. The 1,032 foot-long pier still stands where it started life in 1889 as

McFadden's Wharf, a project of two entrepreneurial brothers. The following year, railroad lines connected the wharf to San Bernardino, Riverside, and Orange Counties, making Newport Beach an important shipping and distribution hub, particularly for building materials making their way to the rapidly developing Inland Empire. 1905 brought the Pacific Electric Railway – the same "Red Cars" that serviced many Los Angeles beaches – which made the trip to Newport Beach an easy one for Angelenos to make. By the time the shipping industry had moved to other ports, Newport Beach had become a hub of the community, with homes and businesses growing up around it.

One of those businesses is the Dory Fleet Market, which got its start in 1891 when, legend has it, a fisherman decided to skip the wholesalers and sell directly to the public on the beach. Today, the Dory Fleet Market is the last remaining beachside fishing cooperative in the United States and is a registered historical landmark. Every morning, the small fishing boats arrive with their catch of the day, which is still sold directly to local restaurants, gourmet markets, and home cooks. Our own daily walks to the pier often included a stroll through the Dory Fleet Market, sometimes to buy but more often to marvel at the spiny, slimy, scaly creatures on display. .

A sea canyon is responsible for the unique wave patterns that make the Newport Pier a favorite spot for surfers and swimmers. The canyon creates a steep drop-off not far from the shoreline; you can dance around with your feet in the sand and dodge the waves in shallow water all day long if you're careful, but if you go one step too far, you're in deep water. It was a rite of passage for us as kids, and no doubt it still is: the day when we were tall, strong, reliable enough as swimmers - and could summon the courage – to venture past the drop-off without a parent right beside us.

Things change, of course. The Pacific Electric rail is long-gone, and affordable little rentals along the beach are a relic of the past. I remember McFadden Square at the foot of the Pier as a confusing cacophony of cars, bicycles, fishing tackle, and wary pedestrians. Now it's an inviting area centered around a bronze monument dedicated to the McFadden brothers, with a maze-like arrangement of pavers that lead visitors through the history of Newport Beach. What hasn't changed is the smell of sunscreen and salt air, the sound of children dipping their toes in the waves, the daily arrival of the Dory Fishing Fleet, the taste of Clam Cooker chowder served in paper bowls, and the feeling of being at home.

A deep sea canyon off of the Balboa Peninsula creates the conditions that make the pier a popular spot for surfers and swimmers.

The Newport Beach Pier offers some of the best recreational fishing in Southern California.

Newport Pier

Balboa Pier

by Debra Branow

Balboa Pier's origin story can be told in just six words: If you build it, they will come. Long before the movie in which Kevin Costner carved his "field of dreams" in the middle of a cornfield, Southern California was a haven for builders and dreamers. In the early years of the 20th century, just such a group bought land on the Balboa Peninsula. Where other saw a narrow, sandy – and largely inaccessible – spit of land, they envisioned summer cottages for people who wanted the best of the beach and the bay. So they they gave Angelenos a reason and a convenient way to make the trek. In 1906, they opened a pier on the ocean side of Peninsula, and a recreational pavilion and bath house on the bay side. At the same time, the Pacific Electric Red Car extended its route, establishing a new southern terminus at the Balboa Pavilion. And the people did come: for a day, for a week, for life. The Newport Bay Investment Company sold its lots within a year of opening the Pavilion and Pier, and the beach cottages started popping up shortly thereafter.

Today, the Pacific Electric line is long gone, and the Balboa Peninsula is only slightly more accessible by automobile than it was in 1906. Balboa Avenue is still the only way to get to the end of the Peninsula and back; the Balboa Island Ferry is a charming alternative, but there's just as much time and traffic involved either way. Though there's no such thing as a "quick trip" to the area, it remains a popular destination for visitors and a beloved home base for residents. It's

the kind of place where indelible memories are made and preserved; much of this area has changed very little since its earliest days.

A visit to Balboa Pier is more than a trip to the beach. It's a feast for the senses with a bit of time travel thrown in. The pier, like many in California, has weathered its share of storms; although the rustic wooden posts, benches and railings have been repaired, replaced, rebuilt and reinforced over the years, they look like they could be the originals dating back to 1906. There is no other smell in the world like the blend of salt water, seaweed, and sunscreen that wafts on the breeze along the concourse: it is the smell of a California summer. At the end of the pier, where the origi-  nal Ruby's Diner serves up 1940s diner fare in the ship-shape little "stream-line moderne" building that was once a bait shop, the smell of burgers and fries takes over.

It's easy to imagine sunbathers and swimmers from every era playing in the waves or perched under umbrellas on the postcard-perfect beaches. For those who'd rather skip the sand between their toes, the beach meets up with Peninsula Park at the foot of the pier, offers groomed lawns and shade trees, an old fashioned gazebo, and a perfect location for flying kites.

A short walk away from the Pier, the iconic Balboa Pavilion still stands. The Pavilion was the end of the line for the Pacific Electric Red Cars, and it provided a convenient place for passengers to change from street clothes into bathing costumes – which were also available for rent at the Pavilion. Boat rentals and sightseeing tours operated from the Pavilion, and still do today. In the 100-plus years since it opened, the Pavilion has been home to the Post Office, a ballroom, a bowling alley and archery range, a bingo parlor, a shell museum, the Newport Harbor Art Museum, various restaurants, and a bait shop. In addition to boat rentals, sightseeing, and sport fishing excursions, the Pavilion now holds the Harborside Restaurant and a ballroom.

Adjacent to the Pavilion, the Balboa Fun Zone has been operating in the same spot since 1936, with many of the same attractions, including the Bay Arcade with old-fashioned SkeeBall and a Ferris Wheel that promises "the longest Ferris Wheel Ride you've ever had." Tucked into the Fun Zone, the Balboa Ferry has been shuttling automobiles and pedestrians to Balboa Island and back since 1919. Finally, fans of the cult favorite television show "Arrested Development" will recognize the Fun Zone as the site of the infamous Banana Stand and various ill-fated activities for the fictional

Bluth family. In fact, a trip to the Balboa Pier and Pavilion isn't complete without a Balboa Bar or a frozen banana, custom-dipped to each customer's specifications. It's the kind of sublime treat that can only exist in a particular context. It cannot be packaged and preserved for another time, and while there may be other places in the world that dip frozen confections in chocolate, they just aren't the same.

Like its namesake confection, there is nothing else in the world like the Balboa Pier, Pavilion and Fun Zone, all squeezed onto a small sliver of the Balboa Peninsula. It takes some patience to get there, but it's worth the trip for the Balboa Bar alone.

Balboa Pier offers amazing views and outstanding dining any time of the day or night at Ruby's. Watch the dolphins swim by, enjoy the beautiful beach or take advantage of the excellent fishing off of the pier.

Balboa Pier

The Balboa Pier was constructed in 1906 as a sister project of the Balboa Pavilion. The Newport Bay investment Company wanted to attract lot buyers to an undeveloped spit of sandy land now called the Balboa Peninsula. In order to do so, they built both the Balboa Pavilion and the Balboa Pier. These two structures were built to coincide with the opening of the southern terminus of the Pacific Electric Railway Red Car line from Long Beach to the Balboa Peninsula. The plan worked; multitudes of beachgoers flocked to Balboa, and many purchased lots.

San Clemente Pier

by Steve Long

In 1925 a visionary by the name of Ole Hanson began selling lots along the coast midway between Los Angeles and San Diego. Creating one of the first master planned communities built on totally open land in the United States, this former Mayor of Seattle had earlier envisioned his "Spanish Village by the Sea, while traveling by train through this virgin coastal zone. The land, once part of a land grant was purchased with the help of Hamilton Cotton, a wealthy industrialist who promptly built his estate and horse racing stables on the southern most promontory of the newly created town of San Clemente, named for the island bearing that name nearly sixty miles offshore.

Attracted by the immediate development of amenities that included roads, restaurants, a community clubhouse, public pool, equestrian trails, parks and a fishing pier, lot sales were brisk, with many celebrities of the day choosing to build their vacation villas in town. An architectural code required all structures to maintain a Spanish Colonial theme and any building that failed to comply with the red tile roof and white stucco requirement was promptly remodeled by the builders or purchased by Ole and his associates who then brought it into compliance.

The 1296 foot" fishing and pleasure pier", as they were often called at the time, was constructed at no cost to the community in 1928. Immediately popular, the pier became the focal point of all beach activities,

San Clemente Pier

including smuggling operations by bootleggers during Prohibition. Ole Hanson built his own hacienda for his family of twelve on the bluff just above the pier and that architectural gem is today known as the Casa Romantica. Sadly, the Great Depression bankrupted Ole and he lost all of his holdings in San Clemente, as the population in the village dropped to 400 from a high above 1200.

The hurricane of 1939 destroyed much of the pier including the café, tackle shop and boat ramp that serviced the "Owl Boat Company" fishing fleet that moored offshore. Several of the boats and a fishing barge anchored in the offshore reefs were destroyed as well. Undaunted, the community rallied and the pier was reconstructed for $40,000 and the fishing fleet quickly returned. The ocean near San Clemente was teeming with life and hauls of albacore, halibut, and white sea bass helped maintain a demand for the seven large vessels that comprised the fleet. Giant Black Sea Bass were also common and local children earned money transporting the catch in their wagons from the boat ramp at the end of the pier back to the parking lot.

During World War II, the land extending for 16 miles immediately to the south of town became a Marine Corps training base. The influx of young Marines bolstered the local economy during the war and many returned following the war to establish homes and businesses. As the southern-most town in Orange County, San Clemente grew slowly but gained national notoriety in 1969 when President Richard Nixon purchased the Cotton estate for his "Western White House." Though the world was now aware of this quaint little coastal village, the days of the fishing fleet operating at the pier were numbered. A small craft harbor was under construction six miles up the coast at Dana Point and by 1971 the fleet was relocated within the safety of the rock jetties.

The "El Nino" winter of 1983 saw massive surf tear 400 feet from the end of the pier and another 80-foot section near the middle. By 1985, 1.4 million dollars in repairs had raised the deck level of the outer end of the pier and fortified the structure with polyethylene coated steel pilings.

Today's San Clemente pier hosts a lifeguard command tower, a tackle shop, restrooms and the ever-popular Fisherman's Restaurant, with open air seating above the surf. The beach and pier draw large year-round crowds with a variety of festivals from Chowder Cook-offs, Classic Car Shows, Lifeguard Competitions and Surfing Tournaments. Fishing will always remain popular. Majestic views and sunsets abound. Visitors from around the world join the residents of San Clemente in thanking Ole Hanson for his vision and gift!

San Clemente Pier is made of wood with spaces in between the wood planks where you can see the water below. The pier offers amazing views of the Coastline and one of the best things about the pier is that the Amtrak/Megtrolink stops here providing beach access to those who travel into the area.

The North side of the San Clemente Pier is a popular surf break. You'll find someone surfing the pier nearly every daylight hour of the year. Greg Long, born and raised in San Clemente began his career here and has become Billabong XXL's most decorated surfer and is regarded as one of the best big wave surfers in the world.

Oceanside Pier

Oceanside Pier

by Sam George

Oceanside's Pride: In the early 1920s a small city located on coast of northern San Diego County adopted an expansive new civic motto: "Oceanside-California's Pride!" And the sleepy seaside berg certainly had plenty to be proud of, with its mild climate, miles of undeveloped beaches and bucolic hinterland. But the city's main source of pride - in fact it's most cherished feature since way back in the 19th century, when the newly coined name "Oceanside" referred to the town's status as an ocean-side resort for wealthy land barons from nearby San Luis Rey Valley - has been its pier. Because with only a precursory look at the city's history it's easy to see that Oceanside has always loved its pier. Why else would they keep rebuilding it over the past 125 years? The first pilings were driven into the sandy bottom in 1888, eventually stretching 1200 feet out into the Pacific at the foot of Couts St. (named for Cave J. Couts, one of the city fathers, since renamed, rather ironically for a beach town, "Wisconsin St.") No commercial structure, the Oceanside Pier was pure spectacle, Then called a "wharf" the wooden pier was a wonder of its age, allowing residents and visitors alike unprecedented (read: safe) access to the wild sea. In the days before ocean bathing was considered anything but eccentric, a stroll out over the plunging breakers was the 19th century version of a theme park, and people from all the surrounding counties thronged the railings, gazing down in awe at the shimmering face of the deep, blue waters over a thousand feet "west of the west."

Trouble was that deep blue sea had another, less accommodating side to its personality. Oceanside's first pier was completed in August, 1888. Warm, mild end-of-summer August, when occasional strong swells generated by far off Southern hemisphere storms would sweep through the pilings with thrilling crash and slash, delighting onlookers, safe on the planking overhead. Imagine the city's dismay when, only months later, the first gales of December raged down from the North Pacific: cold winds, rain and broad-backed, wind-driven monster waves that scoffed at man's feeble attempts at dominion over the shoreline.

Oceanside's pier barely lasted over a year before it was destroyed by a big winter storm in 1890. It was rebuilt — Oceanside needed its pier, loved its pier—this was rebuilt and again, in 1908, the angry sea took it back. Oceanside would not be deterred. The city responded by erecting an even more audacious structure, its pilings and planking stretching a full 1900 feet out into the uncaring sea. The opening, on July 4th, 1927, was like nothing the city had ever seen: three full days of celebration, speeches, fanfare and fun. Oceanside was back and in a big way. The Pride of California again had pride of it's own with its spectacular pier. Then this pier, too, was destroyed in the winter storm of 1942. Following WWII, in 1946 Oceanside fought back in typical fashion, building the West Coast's longest pier (over 1900 ft.) but it was eventually smashed, trimmed back down to size by the relentless winter storm waves.

Yet the city of Oceanside has shown that when it comes to its uneasy relationship with the ocean it is nothing if not optimistic. The current, and sixth, Oceanside Pier is again the pride of the city. Located at the foot of Pier View Way, and completed in 1987, the newest incarnation of pilings and planking remains the town's centerpiece in a way that not even the nearby Oceanside Small Boat Harbor and Marina can match. That impressive feat of coastal engineering presents an entirely different ethic, representing, as it does, a humbling concession to the elements; a place where man and his ships cower behind stone jetties and breakwalls, daring to venture onto the sea only when advantageous conditions allow.

The Pier, on the other hand, exudes a boldness, its very structure stating emphatically that here is a place for people who would live in and around the ocean, if only for the time it takes to walk the 1,954 feet to its distal point in the Pacific. Not just the surfers who for the past 50 years have flocked the sandbar peaks building up on the north and south side; not the generations of fishermen and women who have optimistically dropped their lines off the weathered railing; not the young lovers walking hand in hand and as if on air, life and love's limitless possibilities stretching out before them; not the myriad families with their kids and strollers, crying babies and patient smiles.

Oceanside's pride is about more than what it provides in the way of activities. There's no way that this, the city's sixth pier, would even exist if it didn't represent something more, something deeper that in the spirit of man makes him constantly, and even against insurmountable odds, set his sights beyond the horizon, not accepting the boundaries of anything but the imagination; dreaming, perhaps of what it really feels like to walk on water.

The Oceanside Pier is the best place to surf in Oceanside. Even in summer, Oceanside Pier produces fun and shapely Oceanside waves. Both sides of the pier are popular and on a good day can be quite crowded.

Oceanside Pier

Oceanside Pier is one of the largest wooden piers in California, being 1,942 feet long. This is arguably one of the better piers in the county as far as fishing is concerned. It stretches out into the Pacific from a 3.5 mile sandy beach. Ruby's Diner is located at the end of the pier, offering anglers and visitors a nice place to sit down and enjoy a meal.

Scripps Pier

by Mike Wallace

The Scripps Pier is a private research structure working around the clock for the Scripps Institution of Oceanography (SIO), sampling oceanic conditions, studying sea life, reaching out into the ocean at La Jolla Shores as the invaluable physical arm of the Institution. Small research boats and scuba equipment are housed on the pier and winched in and out of the sea daily. The pier was originally built to pump fresh seawater to the SIO's labs and aquariums. Founded in 1903 as a marine biological station in San Diego, Scripps joined the University of California in 1912 and was renamed the Scripps Institution of Oceanography in 1925, later becoming a department within the University of California at San Diego in 1960.

At Scripps, instead of providing a platform to angle fish from the sea one at a time, the pier provides a window for the Institution of Oceanography's research into the "physical, chemical, biological, geological and geophysical studies of the oceans and earth." One of the oldest and largest institutes of its kind, Scripps has since it's inception been at the cutting edge of teaching and learning about the oceans. Scripps is a leader in the study of a wide range of critical research topics essential to the survival of human race, including marine drug discovery with an emphasis on cancer, climate change, earthquakes, marine biology, pollution, and alternative energy.

The Scripps Institution of Oceanography itself includes surrounding facilities and campus adjacent to the pier, housing 1700 employees who include professors, scholars, researches, students and staff with research awards from institutions such as the Department of Defense, Department of Education, National Aeronautics and Space Administration, National Institute of Health, National Oceanic and Atmospheric and many others. Among them are three Nobel Prize winners, eighteen National Academy of Sciences members and two National Academy of Engineering members.

There has always been a connection between Scripps research and the military, with early developments in wetsuits and SCUBA gear by Scripps researchers for the Navy and anti-mine warfare. Later this equipment took on a life of its own in spreading ocean-faring recreation around the globe. Scripps member and Professor Emeritus at the Institute of Geophysics and Planetary Physics of UCSD, Hugh Bradner, worked on loan to the U.S. Naval Ordnance Laboratory in pioneering research on the wetsuit as a means of keeping Navy SEALS warm and insulated against underwater explosions. He is generally credited with developing the first wetsuit, shortly thereafter commercialized by Body Glove and O'Neill.

Named after the Institute's major benefactor, The Ellen Browning Scripps Memorial Pier was originally constructed of wood in 1915. From its original 1,000-foot span it was rebuilt in 1988 of reinforced concrete to its current 1,084

length and has provided continuous data on the Pacific Ocean since 1916. The pier itself is laced with pipes to pump fresh salt water in and stale out of its terrestrial storage facilities on the cliffs above, including the Birch Aquarium. Gadgets, pumps, fly-wheels, boat launches, docking ladders and other mechanical paraphernalia adorn the pier, testament to its serious scientific purpose. The Scripps campus meanders along La Jolla Shores Drive on down to Discovery Way, which runs right into the pier. Like the climate it studies, Scripps is far from static, with new buildings popping up to house the Marine Ecosystem Sensing, Observation and Modeling Lab (MESOM) and a fully renovated Southwest Fisheries Science Center (SWFSC) Building D, along with a new NOAA wing and J. Craig Venter Institute to boot.

The connection with sea in the Mediterranean-like La Jolla is as strong as the barnacles on the Scripps Pier itself. Like the lithe leopard sharks that migrate to La Jolla's shores to breed each year, the region attracted sea faring families and spawned generations of legendary watermen who went on to pioneer epic surf breaks in Hawaii and around the world. There just seems to be something in the water that breeds larger than life personalities, swashbuckling individualists with an undercurrent of non-conformity verging on arrogance. Unlike the flash and commercialism of Huntington or the low-profile vibe of Santa Cruz, La Jolla's surf culture exudes a history of style-mastery that simultaneously revels in the affluence of the region and rebels against it.

That rebellious culture was embodied by the Windansea Surf Club that was started in 1947 and revived in 1963 to compete at the Malibu Invitational. Among the founding members were luminaries Skip Frye, Mike Hynson, Rusty Miller, Butch Van Artsdalen, Joey Cabell and Rusty Miller, a group that included world-class board shapers, a world champion, a North Shore lifeguard and a founding member of the Chart House Restaurant chain. As founder Chuck Hasley summed it up: "The attitude of Windansea was: 'We're going to win the contest; we're going to dance and take all the girls; we're going to outdrink everybody. And if they don't like it, we're going to beat the shit out of them.'

The Scripps Pier and surf industry in La Jolla share in common a pioneering spirit, a blend of science and style, and an understated bravado born of a passion for the sea. "La Jolla" translates appropriately as "The Jewel," a rare one indeed, which is in safe hands below the surface if the Scripps Institute has its say; while above the surface its surf history and board design contributions have left an indelible mark.

Crystal Pier

by John Fry

When word came that the San Diego streetcar tracks would be extended through Pacific Beach to La Jolla in 1924 Sam Dunaway and Earl Taylor, among others, took notice. Dunaway had come to the beach from El Centro and founded a drugstore on the southeast corner of Cass and Garnet in 1923. Almost immediately he replaced it with a two-story brick building on the northwest corner. His landlord was Earl Taylor, who also arrived in 1923. Convinced a pier at the foot of Garnet Avenue would attract tourists they eventually convinced Ernest Pickering, who had designed piers in the Los Angeles area, to lend his talents to Pacific Beach in return for ocean front property. "Pickering's Pleasure Pier" was still on the drawing board, when Pickering backed away from the project citing financial reversals. Neil Nettleship, a Pickering associate, took over. The pier's opening was held April 18, 1926 even though only the office buildings had been completed. Some of the worst storms of the century prevented the pilings from being towed down from the Northwest and construction of the pier was delayed. The 950 foot long pier, with the Crystal Ballroom at the tip, was officially dedicated on the Fourth of July Weekend 1927 with the promise of "3 Days of Unprecedented Music, Mirth and Merriment!"

The mirth and merriment didn't last long for Neil Nettleship. He discovered, to his horror, that the pier pilings were infested with marine borers and learned that the pilings had not been properly treated with creosote. Nettleship sued and, though winning his case, eventually lost the pier after numerous appeals. The U. S. National Bank fore-closed on the property and set about refurbishing it. No one is quite sure what became of the ballroom, but the pier was lengthened and residential cottages were added where the fun zone once stood. On April 19, 1936 – ten years and one day after its original dedication – Crystal Pier was again open for business.

On January 15, 1953 during a massive storm an out-of-control barge struck the pier. A number of pilings snapped under the force of the collision, and one of the cottages tumbled into the surf. Occupants of the cabin had been evacuated from the cottage two hours before it fell. Their belongings were later recovered.

On Thursday, January 27, 1983 huge storm surf collapsed the pilings at the end of the pier and tore away 150 feet of the decking. Owner Willis Allen, Jr. pointed out that it was a freak combination of waves that struck the end of the pier an up-percut, and tore the decking loose from the tops of the pilings. When the decking was knocked away from the pilings, the end of the pier lost its stability, and a domino-like effect caused the pier to begin to collapse.

A new, shorter pier emerged, and six new cottages were added in 1991. The rest of the '90s were devoted to a massive re-model of the office structure.

The Cottages, built in 1930, have a history of guests enjoying the unique experience of 'Sleeping over the Ocean'.

Crystal Pier is situated on Pacific Beach, which stretches from the Mission Bay jetty to the cliffs of La Jolla and is a favorite area used by surfers year round. A boardwalk runs approximately 3 miles along the beach. There are numerous local shops, bars, and restaurants along the boardwalk, and it is generally crowded with pedestrians, cyclists, rollerbladers, and shoppers.

Crystal Pier

Ocean Beach Pier

by Ed Grant

Ocean Beach Pier was built in 1966 and is one of the most visited landmarks in San Diego County. This was not the first attempt at providing OB residents a place to fish. Prior to the completion of the pier, a bridge had been constructed in 1915 across the mouth of Mission Bay and local fishermen thought they had finally found their sanctuary. Though the bridge served its primary purpose as a means of transportation for local residents, it proved to be a poor solution for the town's fishermen. When the bridge was taken down in 1951, San Diegans were promised a replacement for the tourists and fishermen who enjoyed it.

After 15 years, the city finally came through on its promise and a pier at Ocean Beach was constructed. Local Ocean Beach fishermen were relieved because they needed a way to prevent their fishing lines and lures from getting tangled in the vast kelp and rock beds that lie near the surface of the water near the shores. Now they are able to fish in 25–30 feet of water, staying clear of most of the shoreline kelp and helping them catch a variety of fish that live in deeper waters.

This location at the foot of Niagara Ave. proved better suited for tourists and anglers alike. At 1,971 feet, it holds the record for being the longest concrete pier in the world and it's the second longest pier on the west coast of California. The pier at Santa Cruz is the longest in the state at 2,745 feet. Ocean Beach Pier is T-shaped at the end allowing for two significant extensions. The south branch is 360 feet with a bend at the middle. The north branch is straight and reaches 193 feet to its end.

At the foot of the pier are tide pools that stretch down the coast. These are easily accessible by taking the stairs down to the boardwalk. The way the ocean floor is shaped, as well as the direction the beach faces, means there is great surfing on both sides of the pier, and those surfers are out there in good weather and bad. The pier is the anchor to this fun-loving region of San Diego that enjoys its own logo and identity as an authentic, funky beach town.

Small, encompassing just 1.2 square miles of the City of San Diego, Ocean Beach is wedged between Point Loma to the south and Mission Bay to the north. It's official population count is just under 10,000 but the streets swell with visitor activity most every day of the year. An estimated 500,000 come through here each year to walk the Ocean Beach Pier.

If you're looking for a laid back beach to hang out look no further. Ocean Beach Pier is a favorite among locals who spend their days fishing, surfing, sun bathing, hanging out in their vintage VW vans, and strolling through the many surf shops and antique malls. Ocean Beach offers the perfect throw-back groovy vibe of vintage SoCal, coupled with friendly locals, great dining, and a vibrant night life scene.

Imperial Beach Pier

by Serge Dedina

The Imperial Beach Pier, 1,491 foot-long, stands sentinel over the U.S.-Mexico border and the southern half of San Diego. Located just a few miles north of the Mexican border in the most "Southwesterly City in the U.S.", the wooden pier with Douglas Fir deck planks and steel pilings, juts out into the Pacific and offers sweeping and majestic views of an array of wildlife reserves. From the end of the pier you can view the Coronado Islands in Mexico, the Tijuana Estuary National Wildlife Refuge, Tijuana River Mouth Marine Protected Area, Silver Strand State Beach, and South San Diego Bay National Wildlife Refuge.

On a good day winter day, wildlife viewers can spot gray whales, bottle-nose dolphins, sea lions, harbor seals, and thousands of birds from near-by estuaries feeding on giant bait balls that can extend for over a mile. Birders from throughout the U.S. arrive stroll the pier during the fall and winter with their spotting scopes hoping to catch a glimpse of pelagic migrants in the offshore bird superhighway that connects the pier to the southern and northern ends of the Pacific Flyway.

The Imperial Beach Pier, much like the blue-collar beach town that it is home to, has had a tumultuous history. A wooden pier was first built in 1909 just a couple of blocks north of where the existing pier stands today. Six wave motors designed to power an electric train that brought visitors to Imperial Beach, resulted in the pier being called "Edwards' Wave Motor Pier," after Charles Edwards the designer of the wave motor.

That pier lasted until 1941 when the first of many winter storms that would damage a succession of piers in Imperial Beach, occurred. A new pier was opened the day after John F. Kennedy was assassinated. The popular pier suffered extensive damage in 1969 when large surf knocked out part of the north tee. Later in February 1980, huge waves destroyed a large section of the pier. Hazel Bailey ran the pier concession with her husband Gary back then. "I was out on the pier inspecting the damage when it fell in and barely made it back to the end before the middle section was taken out," recalled Hazel.

That set off a round of reconstruction projects, that due to fierce El Niño-related storms that hit Southern California in the 1980s, never lasted that long. Finally in 1989, the City of Imperial Beach inaugurated the current elegant and classic wooden and steel pier that now stands.

Today a mix of fishermen, locals, tourists and surfers enjoy the Imperial Beach Pier. Fishermen cast their lines out over the surfers who are oblivious to the tourists who watch in awe as surfers perform the latest acrobatic and aerial maneuvers. On big summer swells, surfers sit in a tight pack on the north side of the pier to ride waves that push through the pilings with a loud whoosh and boom. In the winter, large swells can cause surf to break out past the pier on forgotten shoals and reefs.

The pier plaza includes a public sculpture project, Surfhenge, that is a monument to surfers who helped to pioneer big wave surfing at a nearby offshore reef. The open plaza includes a lovely mix of small shops with a French café and ice cream and coffee parlour that offer European style al-fresco dining. On a Sunday summer afternoon, the pier and its plaza fills with families in what is arguably the most culturally diverse and friendliest beach crowd in Southern California.

As a diehard Imperial Beach surfer, I surf up and down the beach of my hometown, but in my heart I will always be a pier rat. The pier is where I feel completely at home. There is something about my connection to those pier pilings that anchors me there and immerses me into a lifetime of vivid and wonderful memories—fishing bonita runs when I was a kid, jumping off the pier to surf my first hurricane swell, and later when I was a lifeguard, leaping out the observation box that spanned both sides of the pier, rescue buoy and fins in hand, to aid swimmers in distress. In the afternoons, I often walk out on the pier and stop right where the water starts and stare out over the Pacific. The pier is my own crow's nest over our "Imperial" beach that draws me back again and again.

The Surfhenge Public Scupture, by Malcolm Jones, has become a beloved symbol of Imperial Beach and functions as the town square.

Looking toward the south side of the Imperial Beach Pier at low tide. During large winter swells waves can break outside the pier. Large storms destroyed parts of the pier in the 1940s, 1960s and 1980s. This current version of the pier was built in 1989.

Imperial Beach Pier

The impressive Sundial stands tall as it commemorates the 88 passengers and crew who lost their lives on Alaska Air Flight 261. The name of each victim is inscribed on the perimeter.

It was a beautiful Sunday morning, a perfect day for a flight down the coast in a new little high performance, pricey Carbon Cub. Just a few minutes south of Oxnard on the coastline looking down, one can see the most interesting and odd zig-zag shape of the Port Hueneme Pier. Can't say it? Try port why-NEE'-me, an Indian name meaning a place of security.

In 1956 a short lived fishing pier was constructed. The Army Corp. of Engineers began pumping in sand for the Channel Island Harbor in Oxnard. That resulted in a widening of the beach and soon the pier sat over sand, not water, making the fishing difficult. The local fishermen, needing a place to fish, together with residents petitioned for renovation and an extension of the existing pier. In 1967 voters approved an $85,000 bond to finance the city's one-fourth cost of the pier (one-fourth came from the county and one-half from the State Wildlife Conservation Board). Construction began on a 1,000 foot extension and renovation of the old pier. The present, odd shaped pier is the result of that work. The pier heads straight out from the beach, turns left for 50 feet then heads straight out again and terminates in a somewhat octagonal shape.

From this unusual pier, on a clear day, one can take in impressive views of the Channel Islands. At the base of the pier, near the gazebo is the Alaska Air Flight 261 Memorial Sundial commemorating the 88 passengers and crew who lost their lives aboard that flight near Anacapa Island in January, 2000. The sundial's bronze dolphins and gnomon cast a shadow on the 20-foot diameter dial face oriented to Pacific Standard Time. Names of each of the victims are inscribed on individual bronze plates mounted on the perimeter of the dial. Anacapa Island is 14 miles offshore. Families of the lost passengers and crew dedicated the sundial as a memorial to loved ones and a work of public art in gratitude to the residents of Port Hueneme for their compassion and tireless assistance in the recovery effort. An investigation by the National Transportation Safety Board determined that inadequate maintenance led to excessive wear and catastrophic failure of a critical flight control system during flight. The probable cause was stated to be "a loss of airplane pitch control resulting from the in-flight failure of the horizontal stabilizer trim system jackscrew assembly's acme nut threads. The thread failure was caused by excessive wear resulting from Alaska Airlines insufficient lubrication of the jackscrew assembly."

Port Hueneme Pier is facing the challenge of protecting it's beaches from erosion and is seeking funding from the Federal government for sand replenishment. This unusual zigzag configuration of the pier was built in an attempt to combat the forces of ocean storms and tides.

When the Port Hueneme Pier opened in 1871, it was the first major pier between Santa Cruz and San Pedro. It was built by the same company that constructed Stearns Wharf in Santa Barbara, as well as piers at Ventura, Gaviota and Santa Monica.

Port Hueneme Pier

Ventura Pier

by Marikay Lindstrom

Let's take a look from aloft at Ventura Pier. May it be from a helicopter, small single engine airplane or by land high above the city from the brim of Grant Park the Pier is truly majestic, picturesque, inviting and approachable. Take your viewing pick, as each offers unforgettable views from above. Flying low over the Pacific shore line approaching this historic pier and depending on the time of day a pilot might feel like making a base leg landing right on to the pier, stopping for that $100 hamburger or in this case a choice of creative tacos, burritos and beer. Or else one might prefer a gourmet leisurely meal with fine wine including the catch of the day as the warmth of the California sun and relaxed pace makes a perfect day. It's all there on the 1,620 foot long wooden pier.

The view from Grant Park, high above the city just to the north is spectacular, especially at sunset. The public road to the park begins at City Hall. It is short, curvy, easy and well-marked. That vantage brings to view the pier as it juts from the impressive shoreline and the picturesque local community. While the setting sun sinks in the west, the colors and shadows on the pier standing strong in the surf take on a whole new panorama.

The Ventura pier originally constructed in 1872 was 1,200 feet in length. In 1914 it was cut in half by the ship the SS Coos Bay and was rebuilt with an addition of 500 feet by 1917. In 1938 it reached in longest length of 1958 feet. The pier has been burned or destroyed by storms numerous times throughout its history. A $3.2 million renovation in 1993 restored its original grandeur. This time the pier was rebuilt using steel pilings for extra support.

Another way to take a look down on the imposing Ventura Pier is from Grant Park, high above the city of Ventura. Looking southward from the Park, the views are spectacular.

Just another beautiful day where paradise can be Ventura Beach.

A little Yoga exercise time on Ventura Beach.

Ventura Pier

Picturesque Ventura Pier offers visitors very casual to fine dining all day long. Its great place to watch the sunset with friends, as well as enjoying a glass of wine or a bottle of beer.

A lone fisherman casts a line into the ocean close to Ventura Pier.

Stearns Wharf

Stearns Wharf is an icon for Santa Barbara, California, a beautiful beach city on the borderline of Southern California and Central Coast California. The most visited landmark in the city offers a unique view of Santa Barbara from the water looking east. In some California cities a view from the pier offers not much to look at except for the sea, but in Santa Barbara, you'll also be treated to something quite special as you gaze to to the lush hillsides framed by stately palms that line the oceanfront.

Considered one of the northernmost beaches in the Southern California region, Santa Barbara was voted as one of the top 10 beaches in the United States by a recent survey. Stearns Wharf is the gateway to State Street, the primary road that contains the heart of the shopping district with access beginning on the north part of the city at a Highway 101 exit, then ending at the base of the wharf where a lovely dolphin fountain welcomes guests gracefully. It's a site befitting this fun, nature-loving city that's home celebrities and regular folks.

First built in 1872, the wharf ranked as the longest deep-water pier between Los Angeles and San Francisco. During that era, bragging rights were crucial in pier size and water depth for getting ships to stop at your location to help promote trade to your town. John P. Stearns worked in the lumber industry and built the wharf for this very reason. With a useful wharf, ships could stop and access the supplies of lumber to be delivered elsewhere. This was the era in which train tracks were still be installed and would one day impact the local port trade both in Santa Barbara and up the coast a short distance in Casmalia. When the railroad finally reached Santa Barbara in 1877, Stearns added an additional spur to the wharf, and later in 1923 that was abandoned as it was no longer of use. A railroad logging car on the spur commemorates the wharf's history.

Frank Quirarte, Guest Photographer

Stearns Wharf has been rebuilt several times after fires have damaged the structure. The most recent event occurred in 1998, and the damaged area was rebuilt while the rest of the wharf remained open.

In its illustrious past, the wharf held many distinctions, not unlike other piers up and down the California coast. From rum runners of the prohibition to gamblers on floating casinos and then to military units standing guard over the coast during World War II (Santa Barbara was the only location where enemy fire actually hit land at the beach near Baraca Resort), Stearns Wharf could tell many great stories if it could talk.

During World War II the Harbor Restaurant was built on the wharf. Opened in 1941, it is still in business today. There are shops, restaurants and great fishing off Stearns Wharf. You can drive your car on the wharf but you must pay for parking which is sometimes limited. The wharf offers fantastic views, great meals, a maritime museum and a bit of souvenir shopping for those seeking good, old-fashioned fun.

Stearns Wharf offers an amazing view of the ocean and all of Santa Barbara.

Princess Cruise line brought the Golden Princess (seen in the distance) to the Stearns Wharf waters for a one day stop. Passengers come ashore for scenic tours on trolleys and on foot to shopping districts, city landmarks and wine country.

Slacklining on the beach at Steans Wharf.

The area offers a multitude of activities for active and passive vacationers: everything from swimming, boating, hiking, and sports fishing to the more exotic jet skiing, kayaking, whale-watching, windsurfing, and horseback riding.

Stearns Wharf

When I was a kid Goleta beach was our go-to beach. My sister and I could ride our bikes there, which meant that we enjoyed a certain level of independence facilitated by a lack of parental supervision. The bike path wound through the backs of neighborhoods and behind the airport, through forbidden, secret areas that weren't accessible from sidewalks.

The journey was always an adventure. There was one scary place on the path that went under a bridge where we often encountered all manners of hooligans and teenaged pot smokers. We were sure that, as long as we rode fast, the bridge trolls couldn't get us. Not that they were really interested.

Once there, we knew that the West side of the beach was going to be filled with UCSB students and the middle of the beach near the Pier was going to be overrun with families and kids taking advantage of the picnic tables and volleyball courts. But the East Side of the beach was the fun side. The East side of the beach was the small expanse of sand between the Pier and the slough. That's where you would find people hanging out in the backs of vans overlooking the ocean, local kids laying on blankets and splashing in the water and people throwing balls for happy dogs running with their tongues hanging out. If the tide was low enough, we could wade across the slough to the deserted part of the beach where it was possible to run into nudists, so we didn't go there much.

After visiting the snack bar at the base of the pier for ice cream bars, we would always end up out on the pier to see what my sister could pull out of the water. My older sister was quite the fishing enthusiast and there was a significant block of time in my childhood when we always traveled with our requisite fishing supplies. We each had a stick about as thick and long as a toilet paper roll, wound the long way with fishing line, with a couple of lead weights crimped onto the line and a fishhook tied to the end, which we stuck into the wood for safety. We never bought bait, we just grabbed a couple of big mussels off of the pilings and smashed them against the planks of the pier with rocks that we had picked up off the beach. No poles, no reels, just good old fashioned hand line fishing with the sticks that my Dad had whittled for us on a camping trip. We would lean against the railing, carved deeply with the initials of generations of teenagers, and watch the water for the line to tighten when a fish took the bait. Usually all we caught were Bat Rays, Brown smooth hound sharks, shovel nosed sharks, guitarfish, and some perch. However, it was endlessly entertaining to see what the water would produce. My sister was fearless in removing the hooks with her bare hands and I thought that she was superhuman for coming away unscathed. Once we caught an octopus, which was a treat and caused quite a commotion on the pier. Whenever we caught something the pelicans and gulls would land all around us on the railing of the pier and I would run at them and wave my arms to keep them away. There were always a handful of crusty fishermen on the Pier, ever hopeful of catching the one big halibut that might wander toward the inshore waters. They mostly kept to themselves until something interesting was caught and then all the denizens of the pier would be magnetically drawn over to our bench to see what we brought out of the water, and more often than not, help us identify the species.

Our visits to the pier seemed incomplete unless we walked all the way to the end. We would walk carefully on the weathered wooden planks in our bare feet, watching the movement of the water far beneath us between the wide cracks. The end of the pier seemed like a dangerous and outlaw place for a couple of young girls. It wasn't terribly pleasant as the fishermen would often clean their catches on the railing at the very tip. The railing would be encrusted with fish blood and scales and bird droppings from the gulls and pelicans that would dive after the fish guts that were released into the sea. We would stand and stare out at the sea. The land seemed far away.

Golita Pier is situated right by the entrance to the University of California Santa Barbara. You can see the university sitting on the bluff overlooking the pier. Looking west, the Channel Islands are clearly visible. A number of signs are put on the pier to educate the public about the tides, marine life and water quality. It is regarded by fishermen as one of the best fishing piers in California A recent fishing report states: "Usually something is biting at this pier and, more often than not, there is an opportunity to catch good quality fish such as halibut, corbina, bass and rockfish not to mention some large sharks and rays."

Gaviota Pier

by Iris King

I woke up on the first morning of March 2014 to the sound of rain and waves pounding the Gaviota coastline from my home. It was an unusual sound to hear one wave after another roaring onshore for this portion of the Santa Barbara Coastline. I got out of bed and looked out from my deck to the ocean. I could see lines of waves stacking up as far as the foggy horizon would let me see. I knew the extreme high tides combined with the high surf was going to make for an interesting day at work.

I am a California State Parks Lifeguard Peace Officer. I have worked on the Gaviota Coast for 11 years and have lived in Santa Barbara County my whole life. That morning, as I was getting dressed for work, I received a devastating phone call from a co-worker saying the end of the Gaviota Pier had been washed away. I knew the storm damage was going to be bad, but I was not expecting such destruction. I drove out to Hollister Ranch Road to get a good view of the pier. As I took out my phone to record the damage, a huge breaker rolled in and snapped a 30 ft.. section clean off the pier. The pier simply snapped as it was a mere toothpick. What I saw at that moment was many memories on that pier just disappear into the ocean; it was truly a sad moment for me.

The Gaviota Pier was built in 1957 to replace the old Hollister Wharf just east of the current pier. When it was initially built, it was only a single land structure for boat and vehicle traffic. In 1967, funds were secured and the pier was upgraded to a double-wide structure with a one ton hoist included for boat launching. It was the only boat launch available for the Gaviota coastline and still is; however, the hoist has now been upgraded to a 3-ton hoist. Since 1957, the Gaviota Pier has been a stoic icon for our coastline. It has withstood decades of heavy winds and winter storms. During its lifetime the pier has endured storm damage and undergone repair and renovations. But the storm damage of the past was miniscule in comparison to the afflictions of the devastation it suffered this year.

I grew up in the small town of Lompoc, and the Gaviota Pier was the first place I learned how to fish. My father took my brothers and me fishing on the weekends using the trusty method of a soda can and fishing line to reel in the "big ones". I never caught more that a bite, but the Gaviota Pier is engraved in my childhood memories and helped to cultivate my love for the outdoors. I began to work for California State Parks when I was eighteen. I began as a park aide working the entrance stations at Gaviota, Refugio, and El Capitan. Every park has its characters, but Gaviota has a special breed of locals and returning campers. The Gaviota Pass can gust anywhere from 30-60 mph winds on any given night. It is a localized climate and if you are not a local with that knowledge, the winds can and will catch you off guard. The visitors that frequent Gav proudly wear a badge of honor for surviving out on the pier during the fiercest of winds to catch their fish. These Gaviota devotees embrace the challenge that the howling winds present to traditional tent camping. There are many mornings when I arrive to Gaviota on my patrol and its not uncommon to see tents in the trash, destroyed by the winds of the night before and weary campers wandering around from a horrible night's sleep. The pier in my mind enjoyed the wind. The wind is part of its home.

The pier has been used for fishing by thousands of fisherman a year. One could always go to the pier and find people fishing no matter the time of day or night. Currently, the pier is destroyed up to where the boat hoist sits. The boat hoist has also been used by hundreds of vessels each year to get to the Channel Islands, Hollister Ranch and the Cojo/Bixby Ranch as well. Park visitors go fishing and surfing from their vessels and the pier has been their platform to get to these idyllic locations as it has been the easiest point of access.

After I was a park aide, I became a seasonal State Lifeguard and earned the title of "Hoist Girl." Boaters were not regulated by the anyone to ensure the proper hoisting equipment was being used and proper safety precautions were being taken while launching boats. As surfing became more popular so did the trek out to The Ranch. Due to the increase in boat traffic it was no longer safe for boaters to launch their own boats and all vessels were required to go through an equipment inspection. I was the lifeguard who was tasked with launching and inspecting these vessels. Being a nineteen year old girl and launching boats for salty fisherman and surfers was not an easy task. They had their ways of doing things, and I was just a little girl in their eyes. It took me a couple of months to earn their respect, but I was able to. I enjoyed my job as the "hoist girl." I would walk up and down the pier everyday and talk to the regulars. I would learn about the amazing culture and history of the pier from the people who lived it. If I were really lucky some of the fisherman would give me some of their catch for dinner.

If the planks of the pier could talk, the stories it could share would be priceless. The community is missing a piece of its livelihood right now. The pier is a piece of our history, but we hope it will be restored and be able to be a piece of our future as well. The lessons I have learned on the pier are lessons I will not be forgetting anytime soon. I am grateful for the time I was able to stand on its deck and take in the beauty of the land I took an oath to protect.

Amtrack's Coast Starlight passes over the trestle at Gaviota State Beach.

Big Waves Destroy Part of Gaviota Pier

On Saturday, March 1, 2014, part of the Gaviota Pier collapsed into the sea after being battered by large waves.

The last 50 feet of the pier was destroyed shortly before 8:30 a.m. "Waves were breaking over top of the pier," according to one observer. "They took out some pilings, and once one goes, they all go down like dominos."

It is estimated that about one-quarter of the pier was demolished. The structure now ends at the location of the boat hoist, often used to launch fishing and Hollister Ranch surf boats.

Above: What the pier looks like now. Below: Gaviota Pier as it looked before the storm.

The Gaviota Pier is perched on top of the oil rich sedimentary rocks of the Monterey Formation. The formation's view provides a south facing landscape of the Channel Islands and oil derricks.

Imagine a small Southern California beach town 50 years ago before Los Angeles metastasized into the sprawling entity it is now? The image in your mind might be similar to the small Central Coast city of Pismo Beach. In some ways, the community even more resembles an unassuming beach town on the New Jersey coast or in the Northeast that can be overrun with tourists during the summer months before becoming a relatively quiet locals' spot when winter takes over.

The true community center of this Central Coast city is its 1,370-foot long pier and the wide, sandy beach that flanks either side of the structure. The city's main drag, Pomeroy Avenue, passes tourist stores, surf shops and seafood joints as it funnels visitors and locals to the pier near the street's end.

The pier is more than just a superb place to get a feel for this beach community; it also is the destination for those who want to enjoy Pismo Beach's prime recreational opportunities of surfing and fishing. On days when the surf is up and the wind is down, surfers take off on watery walls on both sides of the pier. In early summer, an annual event called Wine, Waves and Beyond puts on a surf contest at the pier that raises money for amputee surfers.

The Pismo Beach Pier is even better known as a place to cast a line in hopes of catching a perch or croaker. The structure is the most heavily fished pier on the Central Coast. A concession on the pier deck can rent visiting anglers a pole and bait.

In the 1950s, large Pismo clams could be found in the sand here at low tide. The popularity of the edible mollusk led the community to claim Pismo Beach as the "Clam Capital of the World." Now, due to over harvesting along with a rise in sea otters, which dine on the organism, the Pismo clam is now a rare find on the beach's shorelines even though there is still an annual clam festival occurring every October.

Before a pier was built at the site in 1924, a wharf sat on the sand here beginning back in 1881. The original 1,600 foot long structure was used to ship out agriculture from the region to other markets. When Pismo Beach started to become known as a tourist destination in the late 1800s, a dance pavilion was constructed at the base of the wharf.

The pier as it is today came into being in 1924 though it weathered severe storm damage in 1983. Currently, a walk along the Pismo Beach Pier can take visitors out over the surf to a place in their minds where the beach communities of the California coast have yet to be overrun with development.

Long and wide, the Pismo Pier is an ideal place to take in this section of the Central Coast including the Guadalupe-Nipomo Dunes to the south.

Pismo Pier is a favorite amongst sightseers and surfers who ride the adjacent waves.

Pismo Beach Pier

Port San Luis
Top: Avila Pier; Middle: Cal Poly San Luis Obispo Pier; Bottom: Harford Pier

124

Avila Pier

The scenic Central Coast community of Avila Beach is situated right smack dab on the relatively placid ocean waters of San Luis Bay. The Avila Beach area is unique for having three piers that extend out into the water like stitching connecting the bay to the shore. The three piers are from south to north: the Avila Beach Pier, the California Polytechnic State University Pier (widely known as Cal Poly Pier) and the Harford Pier.

Let's start with the Avila Beach Pier that juts out off Avila Beach's Promenade, which is a block long, pedestrian only avenue of restaurants with outdoor seating. The pier goes out from there over popular Avila Beach, which hosts many sunning beachgoers during the summer months, before heading out into the bay.

The pier was built by the County of San Luis Obispo in 1908. Connected to the northeast end of the wooden pier is the historic San Luis Yacht Club building, which was constructed between 1939 and 1941 by local boat owners. During World War II, the structure was commandeered by the U.S. military for use as a coastal watch lookout. These days, it is used for club events and community get-togethers.

The seaward end of the 1,685 foot-long pier widens so that the whole structure is shaped like a fly swatter. At this side sits Zippy's at the Pier, a blue shack that rents fishing poles and crab nets so that visiting fishermen can attempt to catch the crabs, halibut, mackerel and perch that hang around under the pier. In front of Zippy's is a giant piece of a metal wench that was retrieved from a shipwreck that is buried in 1,335 feet of water.

This end of the pier offers fine views of the scenic nub of headlands to the south known as Fossil Point. Further in the distance, people can take in the tan colored dunes of the Pismo Beach region.

One worthwhile mini-adventure at the seaward side of the pier is to take the stairs down to a metal gangway where small boats can tie up. The gangway offers a different perspective on the manmade structure. Down here, the pilings resemble tree trunks in a dark forest, and balls of barnacles cling to the low lying sections of the pilings like a batch of bee's nests.

Football fans may have seen Avila Beach Pier during the 2010 Super Bowl and not realized it. The pier was the setting of a goofy commercial for Bridgestone that aired between coverage of the game. The 30 second long piece found a trio of young men speeding down Avila Beach Pier in a truck with coverage of the game. The 30 second long piece found a trio of young men speeding down Avila Beach Pier in a truck with a killer whale in back while frantically attempting to return the large creature back to the sea.

Next up, the Cal Poly Pier stretches almost a half-mile out into the bay. Closed to the public, the structure was donated to the local university by oil company Unocal in 2001. Today it is the primary research and lab site for Cal Poly's Coastal Marine Science program, which studies and researches among other topics how to sustain fisheries, how to map ocean currents and how to halt the growth of invasive species.

Possibly the most interesting pier in the region is the Harford Pier, which is the heart of Port San Luis. Home to a small fishing fleet, the protected harbor has fishing boats that bob like oversized plastic bath duckies in the placid waters.

The Cal Poly Pier is home to Cal Poly's Center for Coastal Marine Sciences

Sightseers and fishermen enjoy Avila Beach Pier.

Avila Beach Pier and the adjacent Avila Beach community.

Avila Pier

Harford Pier

by Stuart Thornton

Possibly the most interesting pier in the region is the Harford Pier, which is the heart of Port San Luis. Home to a small fishing fleet, the protected harbor has fishing boats that bob like oversized plastic bath duckies in the placid waters.

Harford Pier was built in 1873 by businessman John Harford. Protruding 2,000 feet into the bay, Harford Pier quickly became a popular cargo shipping structure and passenger transportation hub after its construction. A three-story hotel called the Hotel Marre was created at the landward end of the wharf until a tidal wave wiped it out in 1878. It was rebuilt, and in the late 1880s, a narrow gauge railroad connected the pier to nearby San Luis Obispo. The railroad operated from the pier until 1942.

Today, Harford Pier is home to a diverse range of businesses and activities. B.J.'s Live Seafood operates a unique outdoor seafood market on the structure that sells oysters, crabs and fish. The adjacent Patriot Sportfishing shack is the place to go for booking a day out at sea for a fishing trip or to rent some rods to cast from the pier. There are multiple buildings on Harford Pier in various states of use. Near the end of the pier is a large grey building with an opening in its center that somewhat resembles a giant barn. This was once the old railroad building on the wharf. It is now home to a fish market and the popular Olde Port Inn. Despite its name, the Olde Port Inn is not a place of lodging but a popular seafood restaurant.

Of note are two islets that can be viewed from Harford Pier: Whalers Island and Smith Island. Looking like not much more than barren rocks in San Luis Bay, the two islets have actually hosted significant human activities in the past. Whalers Is-

land is connected to the breakwater now, but it was once an active whaling station. The nearby Smith Island somehow managed to sustain to three families for a period of time.

The native people used to refer to Avila Beach as a place with "a hole in the sky" due to the fact that the region could be frequently sunny when the surrounding area was fogged in. Now a thriving beach community, Avila Beach is a worthy Central Coast stop especially for visitors who want to take in the coastline from the Avila Beach Pier and the Harford Pier.

The Harford Pier in Avila Beach was developed in 1873 by John Harford for shipping into San Luis Obispo before the train came. It was also used by smugglers at nighttime for illegal movement of liquor. Now, the Harford Pier is a great spot for fishing, commercial fishing and dining, or simply enjoying the view.

The historic Cayucos Pier stretches out from the coastal community of Cayucos with Morro Rock towering in the distance.

Caycucos Pier

by Stuart Thornton

Cayucos might be the quintessential California beach town. There are no roller coasters here or any other real attraction to divert your attention from the surf and sand. This isn't a fancy resort town, but rather a place people come to for sitting in the sand, plunging into the Pacific and just being soothed by the sound of surf.

The real must-see sights of Cayucos are the beach and the pier that protrudes from its town center. The wood pier offers views of the popular beach, which is frequently decorated with strands of kelp, the hills to the east and the distinctive mound of Morro Rock to the south.

The pier itself is intricately intertwined with the history of Cayucos. The structure was constructed in 1872 by Captain James Cass, who was also the town's founder. (The nearby Cass House Inn and Restaurant was where the captain lived.) Rebuilt in 1876 with wood from nearby Cambria's pine trees, the pier became an essential Central Coast shipping spot, where items produced in San Luis Obispo County including butter and milk were transported to other locales. In 1915, an abalone canning plant was built on Cayucos Pier.

Today, the warped wooden deck of the pier is a nice place for a stroll and a prime place for catching snapper, trout and halibut. Due to years of neglect and pounding storms, the Cayucos Pier is in jeopardy of becoming a thing of the past like the town's prominence as a shipping destination. The Cayucos Pier Project (www.save-cayucospier.org) is working with San Luis Obispo County to raise funds to save this low-key landmark.

Cayucos Beach and Cayucos Pier are the heart of this coastal community.

The Cayucos Pier Project hopes to restore the dilapidated seaward end of the pier.

Cayucos Pier

San Simeon Pier

by Stuart Thornton

Above San Simeon Cove and the 795-foot long San Simeon Pier, the Hearst Castle, the opulent mansion of newspaper magnate William Randolph Hearst, crowns a small coastal mountaintop. It's a fitting image because the Central Coast landmark basically dominates the area's economy and is the reason that the town of San Simeon still exists today.

The cove was the site of a small whaling industry in the mid 1800s. In 1864, Captain Joseph Clark built a pier by San Simeon Point, which is located just north of the current pier. But that pier was unusable during heavy seas so a new wharf was built in 1878 by George Hearst that was better protected by the long arm of San Simeon Point.

The current pier's first incarnation was in 1957 as a 495-foot long structure before being extended to 795 feet in 1969. The Hearst Corporation donated the San Simeon Pier to San Luis Obispo County in 1953, and then in 1970, the structure and its surrounding land was given to the California Department of Parks and Recreation. Today it is a part of W.R. Hearst Memorial State Beach.

These days, the narrow, wooden structure is a place for fishermen to try and catch a perch or croaker. It is probably used even more by visitors to view the area's understated natural beauty before or after touring the Central Coast's best known manmade feature: the nearby Hearst Castle.

Walking distance of the pier is Sebastian's Store, a historic building dating back to the late 1800s that currently houses the San Simeon Post Office, Hearst Ranch Winery Tasting Room and a small café that serves amazing burgers made from Hearst Ranch beef.

Beachgoers on William Randolf Hearst Memorial State

The short San Simeon Pier is a good place to take in one of the Central Coast's most tranquil coves.

Monterey Wharfs

Monterey Wharves

Monterey has three wharves including one on each end of its scenic harbor that embrace the sailboats and fishing boats from the open waters of Monterey Bay. Each of the three offers up different experiences. The most popular, Old Fisherman's Wharf is a former working wharf transformed into a tourist destination known for its summer crowds, caricature artist, clam chowder restaurants and its outgoing whale watching vessels.

The Coast Guard Pier is really just a breakwater, but this usually uncrowded structure offers fine views of the harbor and the vibrant harbor seal colony at its tip. Meanwhile, understated Municipal Wharf II has working seafood operations that offer a glimpse into Monterey's fishing past and, possibly, its future.

Old Fisherman's Wharf is frequently covered with a blanket of people on summer weekends. The visitors are handed sample scoops of clam chowder by employees standing in front of competing seafood restaurants as they pass by the wharf's gift shops where they can purchase sea otter adorned T-shirts or other Monterey souvenirs. The Old Fisherman's Wharf also has a variety of seafood restaurants. The best of the batch is Abalonetti Bar and Grill, which is known around town for its calamari. They do the typical fried calamari, but they also whip up some unique takes on the squid including one that is similar to the recipe for Buffalo chicken wings.

The Old Fisherman's Wharf is home to an uncommon business for most wharves and piers: a theater. One version of the Bruce Ariss Wharf Theater opened back in 1950 though a fire destroyed it in 1959. The theater officially returned to the wharf in 1976 with a production of Guys and Dolls. Today, the Bruce Ariss Wharf Theater puts on sporadic plays like Gilbert and Sullivan's Pirates of Penzance.

Old Fisherman's Wharf used to be a grittier, working wharf for the fishing industry before it was transformed into a tourist destination after World War II. It was initially constructed as a passenger and freight transport facility in 1845. As the local sardine industry blossomed, the Monterey City Council took over the wharf in 1913. By 1920, it was an important spot for local fishermen with a marine service station, several retail fish outlets and an abalone shell grinding business.

Though Monterey became a serious sardine provider for the rest of the world—see John Steinbeck's 1945 novel Cannery Row—the burgeoning business was not without mishaps. On March 3, 1923, the S.S. San Antonio was tied to the wharf and ready to be loaded down with the largest amount of sardines ever shipped from Monterey (20,000 cases). But bad weather caused the boat to tip over onto the wharf resulting in 132 feet of the pier collapsing and 10,000 cases of sardines being returned to the sea.

History buffs should consider signing up for a wharf history walk with local historian Tim Thomas. The walks take place the first Saturday of every month at 10am. Call (831) 521-3304 for reservations.

When Monterey's sardine industry began to collapse, the Old Fisherman's Wharf wisely turned to another way of making money: tourism. By 1956, it was home to candy stores, gift shops, restaurants and an aquarium, which is no longer there.

Nearby **Monterey Municipal Wharf II** is the overlooked stepbrother of the far more popular Fisherman's Wharf. Yet, this structure reaching out from the eastern edge of Monterey Harbor offers terrific glimpses into Monterey's seafood industry's past—and possibly its future. Its busy tip extending out into the water is a place where fishing boats still unload their catch and ship it out to local and regional restaurants. It feels more like the Monterey described in Steinbeck's Cannery Row than the other touristy wharf.

Located at this seaward end of the wharf, the Monterey Fish Company and Royal Seafoods sell wholesale seafood to those who venture out on this underrated gem of a structure. Between these two unassuming storefronts is the Monterey Abalone Company, which runs an abalone farm under the wharf. This sustainable aquaculture operation may very well be the business of the future.

The business is one of just 10 abalone farms on the California Coast. It cultivates from 100,000 to 500,000 California red abalones from the size of a pinky fingernail to six inches. On the dark gangways under the wharf, employees of Monterey Abalone bring in kelp from Monterey Bay to feed the abalones, which are on panels in cages that dangle down into the green waters below. The nearby pilings are cloaked in pink anemones that resemble natural leggings and testify to the health of the restored bay.

The seafood companies are just one aspect that makes the Municipal Wharf worth a visit. Its eastern side is popular with anglers hoping to catch mackerel or sardines. It is also home to LouLou's Griddle in the Middle—a micro diner that serves seafood based breakfast specials along with lunch and dinner—and the Sandbar and Grill, a seafood restaurant that hangs off of the wharf over the adjacent harbor. In addition, the wharf peers out on the golden expanse of Del Monte Beach and its placid waters that is popular with stand-up paddle boarders and kayakers.

Sheltering the Monterey Harbor from fierce storms arriving from the north, the Coast Guard Pier was initially built as a 170-foot long breakwater in the 1930s by the U.S. Army Corps of Engineers. It was later transformed into a wharf, which provides access to for the local Coast Guard to their fleet. The structure is known as a fine place to take in sea lions, harbor seals and sea otters. In addition, the section of water northwest of the Coast Guard Pier is a popular SCUBA diving spot, and visitors can see beginner divers' heads surfacing and disappearing in the waters like the plastic figurines in the old Whac-A-Mole arcade game.

All in all, Monterey's three wharves offer and afternoon of activity while providing a variety of vantage points to take in Monterey Harbor's picturesque beauty.

Seacliff State Beach Pier

by Stuart Thornton

The wide, wooden pier of Seacliff State Beach has something that no other piers on the California coast have: a sunken ship on its seaward side. That vessel is the 435-foot long Palo Alto, which was built in Oakland in 1919 as a tanker for World War I. When the war ended before the boat was completed, the concrete vessel was bought by the Seacliff Amusement Company and towed to Seacliff State Beach, where it was settled on the sea bottom for use as an "amusement ship."

For two seasons, the ship's deck was flooded with visitors. Some came for the Rainbow Ballroom's large dance floor, which was 156 feet long and 54 feet wide. Others came for the seafood meals and fine views served up by the onsite restaurant, the Fish Palace.

Unfortunately, after those two successful seasons, the Palo Alto and the Seacliff Amusement Company had to deal with some unexpected squalls. The first was an actual storm that cracked the concrete ship's haul. The second was the financial downturn known as the Great Depression, which helped cause the Seacliff Amusement Company to collapse.

The great concrete vessel was thankfully bought by the California State Parks in 1936 for just one dollar. Though the Palo Alto continued to deteriorate over the years, it remained intermittently open to the public until it was closed down permanently in 2000.

Today, the Palo Alto's deck resembles a construction site with broken concrete slabs and twisted metal. One can get real close to it on the wooden pier though a locked gate prohibits access to the vessel.

These days, it's wildlife that enjoys the Palo Alto the most. Pelicans and cormorants use it as a perch. In the summer and fall, clouds of small seabirds called sooty shearwaters darken the skies over the boat. Mussels, barnacles, sea stars and anemones decorate its sides.

The state pier leading out to the Palo Alto is popular with fishermen. They attempt to catch some of the sole, flounder, mackerel, halibut, lingcod and the occasional salmon that swim around the ship's remains. The pier has fish cleaning stations and a fish species display for visiting anglers.

Behind the pier is a nub of land with a picnic area under the bluffs of Seacliff. In addition, there is a little visitor center just a few hundred feet from the base of the pier. Though small, the interesting visitor center has a model of the Palo Alto, a red tailed hawk display and a small viewing tank filled with tide pool organisms including anemones, urchins, starfish and a prickleback fish.

Above the beach, there is a popular RV only campground. The sites offer views of the mile-long beach below and Santa Cruz, which is five miles north.

Seacliff State Beach looking northwards to Santa Cruz.

The skeletal remains of the Palo Alto.

Young people participating in the California State Park Life Guard Program.

From Seacliff State Beach Pier looking towards the state park's coastal bluffs.

Jutting 855 feet into the (usually) placid Pacific from the seaside hamlet of Capitola, the Capitola Wharf offers fine views of the Santa Cruz County coastline. To the left of the seaward end of the wharf, mooring buoys float on the water like oversized fishing bobbers. Looking the other way, one can see the white lines of waves breaking off the popular surf spots of Pleasure Point.

Peering towards shore, Capitola Beach is splayed out in front of the seaside village like a giant golden blanket. Among the notable buildings behind the beach is the brightly colored Venetian Court, which is now a motel but opened as a unique cluster of townhouses in 1925.

The Capitola Wharf offers more than nice scenery though. Operated and maintained by the City of Capitola, the wharf is home to Capitola Boat and Bait, which has 15-foot wooden skiffs for rent. The brightly colored red and green boats are lowered into the water by a hoist on the wooden pier.

The store also rents out rod and tackle for anglers attempting to catch one of the bullheads, kingfish, perch, skates or sharks from the waters below. Photos of people with impressive catches are plastered on the store walls revealing that there are definitely some fish to be caught in this area.

The other business on the structure is the Wharf House Restaurant, which serves up what you'd expect — fried calamari, fish and chips — in a nautically decorated interior. Seasonally, the outside upper deck of the restaurant opens on weekend afternoons for dining, drinking and live music.

One interesting feature of the wharf are the numerous bronze memorial plaques that adorn its wooden guardrails. The plaques commemorate lost loved ones who cherished the wharf, whether they were local or from out of town. Some of the plaques have the individual's name along with an inscription. One inscription at the end of the wharf reads: "I am wild and dangerous yet delicate as the pale blue shell of a robin's egg."

Dating back to 1857, the wharf has a rich history. The initial structure was built by Sedgwick Lynch and Frederick Augustus Hihn. The latter owned the land that would later become the town of Capitola. Freighters from a steamship company utilized the wharf in the late 1800s, and a colony of Italian immigrant fishermen sprung up at the base of the structure. In 1913, a 200-foot section of the wharf's midsection was washed away by storm surge. The sudden event stranded a

fisherman named Alberto Gibelli on the still standing ocean end of the wharf that was now disconnected from shore. Gibelli was eventually saved by a fellow fisherman in a boat who tossed him a rope and a life preserver. Later, high tides in 1983 wiped out a 30-foot span of the wharf.

The wharf had several owners before the city took over control of the structure. One of its owners for a time was major league baseball player Harry Hooper, who played as an outfielder for the Boston Red Sox and the Chicago White Sox. The National Baseball Hall of Famer was the first player to hit two home runs in a single World Series game.

The adjacent town of Capitola was once the site of an old Indian village. In 1874, a seaside camp opened in the spot calling itself "Camp Capitola." In later years, the camp was transformed into a resort village with hot water salt baths and the Hotel Capitola. Built in 1895, the Hotel Capitola was a resort known for its ballroom with a concert stage and glass enclosed clubhouse before it burned' down in 1929. Capitola became a city in 1949, and it is now a favorite place for visitors craving the beach, sun and its small walkable downtown. The Capitola Wharf is still an integral part of the beach community after all of these years. It is a site for annual events including the Capitola Wharf Fishing Derby and the Wharf to Wharf, a six-mile footrace from Santa Cruz Wharf to Capitola Wharf that occurs in late July.

Capitola Wharf

The kelp strewn Capitola Beach with Capitola Wharf in the background.

Departed loved ones are remembered on Capitola Wharf with bronze plaques and flowers.

Capitola Wharf from the bluffs above.

A surfer hops off Capitola Wharf en route to a nearby break.

Santa Cruz Municipal Wharf

by Mike Wallace

Santa Cruz has a chip on its shoulder and rightly so. It has arguably one of the best set-ups for surfing in the state, yet it has second-class citizenship in the eyes of the L.A.-centered surf industry. Surfing talent runs as deep in the sleepy, laid-back, Northern Californian burgh as its proliferation of point breaks and reefs. In some ways this suits its low-profile surf citizenry, in others it's a cause of frustration.

This may be at the root of its reputation as an incubator for surly localism with the archetypal grumpy old guy regulating the line-up out the back and hot-tempered young rippers slashing and burning on the inside. While that reputation can still rear its head, it has been tempered somewhat with the gentrification of the region that spilled over from Silicon Valley. This contrasts with the grittier blue collar roots of the region that still bubbles beneath the surface. Yet, kids, wives, dads and grand-dads populate marquee breaks like Pleasure Point and Steamer Lane and points in between, cooling tempers somewhat and defusing some historic tension. Former hot heads and rippers more often than not have their own kids and spouses in the line-ups and hostility is less of a factor, though that's not to say a pecking order doesn't exist, especially on the best days and more heavily regulated spots.

The Santa Cruz Wharf itself is an apt symbol of this low-pro vibe and the longest pier in the state; it has none of the pomp and glitz of Huntington and other SoCal piers. Low, wooden and practical, it wears its attitude on its timbers like a tightly pulled-down baseball cap and sunglasses favored as the surf uniform of choice by locals.

First mainland spot surfed in the United States was believed to be the San Lorenzo

Rivermouth near today's boardwalk by a trio of Hawaiian princes on break from military school in San Mateo.

The Monterrey Bay's South-westerly orientation and deep kelp beds guarantee groomed surf more often than not, with southwest winds the only exception to this rule. This ensures that a hot bed of high performance surfing incubates with repeatable moves in its wave-machine-like points.

Until recently, it hasn't had Hollywood backing it – "Chasing Maverick's" changed that, but making a "G-rated" movie about growing up in Santa Cruz should've earned an Academy Award for just pulling that off.

Surf Industry took root in Santa Cruz when Jack O'neill relocated his budding wetsuit business and the first "Surf Shop" from chilly San Francisco to more temperate Santa Cruz in 1959.

The Wharf has a long history as a working pier, the last survivor of several built in the early nineteen-hundreds that included the Potato Wharf, Railroad Wharf, Powder Mill Wharf and Pleasure Pier. Shipments of supplies for the Gold Rush in the Sierras were launched from these platforms. Today whale watching expeditions, fishing charters, cruises and kayaking all embark from its pilings.

The Santa Cruz Beach Boardwalk opened in 1907, making it California's oldest surviving amusement park and one of the best seaside amusement parks in the world. The low-profile Wharf is unusual as one can drive out upon its wooden slats and park in order to enjoy its eight restaurants, six snack bars and one wine tasting bar.

The Wharf has a long history as a working pier, the last survivor of several built in the early nineteen-hundreds that included the Potato Wharf, Railroad Wharf, Powder Mill Wharf and Pleasure Pier. Shipments of supplies for the Gold Rush in the Sierras were launched from these platforms. Today whale watching expeditions, fishing charters, cruises and kayaking all embark from its pilings.

Surfers enjoy sharing a soft roller heading into Cowell's Beach just to the West of the Wharf. Good vibes abound in this classic beginner spot, abundant as the kelp and foam-top surfboards.

Woodies, Surfing and Woodies on the Wharf

by Don and Cathy Iglesias

Back in 1993, we never would have imagined that the bringing together of woodies and their families, through the creation of the Santa Cruz Woodies Car Club, would have created the lasting friendships and memories that define the group. Since the beginning, the club has focused on the historical significance of woodies in the sport of surfing. We have grown from a small core group of Santa Cruz surfers into a statewide and beyond group of wooden car enthusiasts with over two hundred members.

Our collaborative partnership with the city of Santa Cruz culminated in the summer of 2014, at the 100th anniversary of the Santa Cruz Municipal Wharf and the twentieth anniversary of "Woodies on the Wharf."

For all of us in Santa Cruz Woodies, the love of woodies has been a passion that ignited the first time we fired up the old bombs and lurched down the street. For many of us, the linkage to funky old surf cars in the 60s and the simpler times we all enjoyed are brought back every time we climb into our cars. For others, it is the love and uniqueness of driving a wooden car. Woodies stand out among all cars, wherever they travel. They were destined to be dinosaurs from the beginning; being totally impractical and like "a piano on wheels."

Personally, our '49 Mercury Woodie has been a part of our family since the first time it belched its way into our driveway twenty-five years ago. My personal love of woodies started as a little kid in the back of my dad's 1951 Ford Country Squire. I still remember the smell of the car and the noises it made as we traveled throughout California. During the summer, the car always made it to the Santa Cruz' Sky-View Drive-In, packed with little kids in pajamas, watching "Ma and Pa Kettle" or the "Creature of the Black Lagoon".

In 1993, a group of local woody lovers and crusty Santa Cruz surfers, got together and decided to form Santa Cruz Woodies. Since its inception it was always about family and spouses and kids. In the beginning it was just a few cars and the simple idea that people and friendship were always more important than the cars.

Back in the day, our cars leaked their bodily fluids and were held together with duct tape and bailing wire. At the first club meeting, we joked about buying a tow truck for the club, because half of our cars kept breaking down. The club always had a connection to surfing and the beach lifestyle at its core. For all of us in the Santa Cruz Woodies, from the beginning until now and into the future, we hope that the soul of Santa Cruz Woodies stays healthy and focused on the parts of life that really matter; friends, families and funky old wooden cars.

Here's to another twenty years of cruising!

Two Gulls stand vigil over the Sanctuary sign on the Santa Cruz Wharf, which looks South toward Cannery Row in Monterey. Similarly, the Monterey Bay National Marine Sanctuary stands guard over this protected marine reserve that runs some 276 miles of shoreline from Marin to Cambria and extends some 4,601 square nautical miles into the Pacific. The MBNMS was dedicated in 1992 as a federally protected area, with the aim of promoting environmental protection, stewardship and ocean research. Sometimes you have to head to sea to visit the Sanctuary's famed wildlife and sometimes it comes right to you.

The Sea Odyssey - A Living Classroom

In 1996 Jack O'Neill, the wetsuit innovator, created a living classroom on board this 65-foot catamaran. It sails the Monterey Bay National Marine Sanctuary with 4th - 6th grade students who receive hands-on lessons about the marine habitat and the importance of the relationship between the living sea and the environment. "What we're doing with the Sea Odyssey is the most important thing you can do today," says Jack O'Neill, "It's something we can do to help save the planet." As of December 3, 2013, 75,000 students have passed through the program.

Pacifica Pier

Pacifica Pier

by Frank Quirarte

In 1973 the City of Pacifica, the Wildlife Conservation Board and the California Department of Fish and Game designed and funded a concrete, open-ocean L-shaped pier extending nearly a quarter mile out to sea. The pier, located at the north end of Pacifica, is one of the defining landmarks of the sleepy coastal San Francisco suburb.

The Rev. Herschell Harkins Memorial Pacifica Pier was originally built as a support structure for the city's now obsolete sewer pipe, but the efforts of the men who routinely placed themselves in danger erecting the structure are the real unsung heroes of the project. In 2004 the city relocated and upgraded its water treatment plant near the south end of town, and with the sewer pipe now gone, the area has become more of a tourist destination and one of the best sport fishing platforms in California. Highlighted in numerous fishing blogs and articles, it is famous for its salmon runs and winter Dungeness crabbing and attracts anglers from around the globe.

Unlike other piers along the California coast, with their boardwalks and lifeguard towers, the Pacifica Pier is not quite as romantic. It had to be built to withstand the fury of Northern California winter storms and their 20-foot waves. Given the tide, the pier sits in roughly 25 to 30 feet high on a calm day. It's built almost totally of reinforced concrete and steel with the main pilings buried deep into the ocean floor. There are no structures actually on the pier, and it has no color other than the gunboat grey of concrete.

Nevertheless, over the years the pier has provided tourist and locals with a spectacular show of man-against-nature, withstanding giant 30-foot storm surf that sometimes crashes completely over the structure. If you happened to be on the pier before they closed the gates you could feel the entire pier resonate under your feet. Giant waves crashing down the side and over the top drench the fearless that venture out during a big storm. There doesn't seem to be any clear guidelines on when they close the gates near the entrance of the pier, but given the age and wear on the pier, most any large surf with stormy conditions will now trigger a closure.

Not all big waves come with storm conditions and they don't always close the pier on days with big surf. Like other famous piers, it happens to sit on top of one of Pacifica's popular surfing breaks. On any given day a few brave local surfers will run out to the end of the pier, throw their boards over the edge and then jump in. On the right wave it's possible to actually surf through the pilings below. But should a surfer get caught "shooting the pier" they pay a hefty fine to the local authority. This sort of behavior is highly frowned upon.

The pier doesn't host annual dedication ceremonies, parties and festivals on its salty decks. It now just sits as a monument of engineering to all who visit. It has withstood over 40 years of relentless abuse from the North Pacific, weather and visitors. Hopefully it will be there for future generations to come.

Pacifica Pier is a famous fishing pier that has been called the best fishing pier in the state. On one occasion, for example, as many as 1,000 salmon were landed in a single day. So many fish were landed in fact, that the Fish and Game deputies finally came out to the pier to check on the action. Most notable was the citation to one angler who had caught 17 salmon all by himself – which is about 850% of the 2-fish limit.

Frank Quirarte, Guest Photographer

There are many great surfers in this region and Mavericks, the world famous surf break, is located just a few miles to the sound in Half Moon Bay.

Pacifica Pier

Point Arena Pier

by Stuart Thornton

On a summer night, a year ago, I stood on the Point Arena Pier at midnight and was totally in awe of my surroundings. Above, the stars burned brightly and the Milky Way was a noticeable smear across the sky. Below the stars, cliffs on either side of the pier cupped the cove's placid waters. But, I was most struck by how the pier and Point Arena Cove were a little known spot along the California Coast. This was an amazing and unique place that not many knew about.

The pier is a concrete and steel structure sticking out in the cove a paltry 330 feet. Point Arena Cove had a wharf as far back as 1866, and in the 1870s, it was allegedly the most active North Coast port between San Francisco and Eureka. The new concrete and steel version of the pier was constructed after the fierce winter storms of 1983 reduced the old wooden pier to splinters.

While the small city of Point Arena's main street is a section of Highway 1 a mile from the ocean, Point Arena Cove feels like the true center of this coastal community. The cove is a hangout for local fishermen, abalone divers and surfers who seem to be constantly gauging the fishing conditions, water conditions and surfing conditions.

A two-story building a few feet back from the Point Arena Pier is home to the Pier Chowder House and Tap Room on the top floor and the Cove Coffee and Tackle Shop on the bottom floor. A little further from the water with views of the cove are two places to stay: the Wharf Master's Inn and the Coast Guard House. The latter was a former Coast Guard Life Saving Station that has now been transformed into a cozy bed and breakfast.

The pier itself has restrooms, showers and fish cleaning facilities. It is also known as a superb spot to cast a line for perch, greenling and cabezon. There is even the possibility of catching a rogue salmon during some times of the year.

The near perfectly shaped cove is located a mile and a half south of Point Arena, a bulge on the coast that is closer to the islands of Hawaii than anywhere else on the state's coastline due to its extreme western position. The point itself is home to the 115-foot high Point Arena Lighthouse, the tallest lighthouse on the west coast.

A mile northeast of the cove is the tiny city's Main Street, which is a section of Highway 1. The strip has the popular Arena Market and Café along with the Point Arena Theater, a venue dating back to 1929 that currently hosts first run movies, performances and community events.

The short Point Arena Pier is a perfect spot to marvel at this underrated strip of the California coast and one of the highlights of the small city of Point Arena.

The locals are fiercely protective of Point Arena's waves.

The small Point Arena Pier juts out from a small cove.

Trinidad Pier

by Stuart Thornton

The tiny town of Trinidad is one of California's most scenic coastal communities. Just 15 miles north of Arcata, Trinidad, which is one of the state's smallest incorporated cities (population: 360), overlooks a small, scenic bay studded with rocky islets and moored fishing vessels.

Sheltered from the north by Trinidad Head, a rocky promontory, Trinidad Pier reaches 520 feet out into the distinct natural harbor area. The wooden pier, which was here until a couple of years ago, was constructed in 1946 with funds from the Arcata Lumberjacks' Association.

After an $8.3 million reconstruction, a new pier consisting of a concrete deck held up by steel pilings was unveiled in July of 2012. While the old wooden pier had creosote wooden pilings that were feared to be contaminating nearby kelp beds, the new eco-conscious structure has been designed so that rainwater doesn't wash oil and other contaminants into the sea.

Trinidad Pier is home to one of the Trinidad's most popular annual events: The Blessing of the Fleet. Every Thanksgiving morning on the pier, Native American and Christian prayers are said in an attempt to protect local fishermen from harm.

Another attraction on the pier is the long running Seascape Restaurant. The initial eatery was swept away by a storm in 1959, and the current unassuming home-style restaurant was constructed a year later. Its current menu includes a local breakfast oddity: scrambled eggs drenched in clam chowder. During summer, sport fishing vessels take off from the pier, while the winter finds commercial crabbers scampering about on the concrete structure. For those not willing to cast their own line, head up the hill to Katy's Smokehouse, where you can get a taste of the sea with some mouthwatering slabs of smoked salmon.

Fishing boats cluster around Trinidad Pier.

Commercial crabbers and local fishermen utilize Trinidad Pier.

The Trinidad Memorial Lighthouse stands vigil over those lost at sea.

Crescent City is the end of the line. The northernmost city on the California coast, Crescent City is also the only incorporated city in sparsely populated Del Norte County. This used to be timber and commercial fishing country though both industries are not what they once where resulting in Crescent City's current day ghost town-like feel.

Crescent City was first established in 1853 and quickly became a supply and trading center for area gold miners. In the following years, the timber industry grew and was the main financial support before logging experienced a significant downturn after 1950.

The topography of the sea floor off Crescent City is ideal for creating tsunami conditions. On March 7th, 1964, the 9.2 Richter scale Good Friday Earthquake off of Alaska sent four massive waves into Crescent City that destroyed 30 city blocks and killed 11 people. More recently, tsunami tidal waves caused by the Japanese earthquake of 2011 resulted in massive damage to the city harbor and dozens of boats in addition to the death of one person.

B Street Pier is located on the north end of the Crescent City Harbor and faces south. It is protected from rough seas by a long hockey stick shaped jetty. The 720 foot long pier was opened in 1989 after the Dutton Wharf was demolished in 1988.

The pier is popular with anglers who cast their lines into the water hoping for perch, jacksmelt, sand dabs and halibut. It has also become a spot for recreational crabbers casting out and hauling in pots of Dungeness crab.

For sightseers, the B Street Pier offers fine views of the nearby Battery Point Lighthouse, a scenic red and white light station located on an island that is only connected to the mainland on extreme low tides. First illuminated back in 1856, the lighthouse withstood the tidal waves of the 1964 tsunami.

Tours of the lighthouse, which are only available at low tides, include a look at maritime artifacts and a climb up into the light tower for views of the remote Crescent City coastline. If you are in town only during high tide, head out to B Street Pier to snap some photos of the one-of-a-kind lighthouse.

Crescent City's B Street Pier with the wild North Coast in the background.

The B Street Pier offers a close-up view of Crescent City's harbor area.

Piers of the California Coast - Length In Feet

#	Pier	Length
1.	Santa Cruz Municipal Wharf	2,745
2.	Ocean Beach Pier	1,971
3.	Stearns Wharf	1,950
4.	Oceanside Pier	1,942
5.	Huntington Beach Pier	1,856
6.	Seal Beach Pier	1,835
7.	Coast Guard Pier, Monterey	1700
8.	Avila Beach Pier	1,685
9.	Municipal Pier #2, Monterey	1636
10.	Ventura Pier	1,620
11.	Imperial Beach Pier	1,491
12.	Goleta Pier	1,450
13.	Port Hueneme Pier	1,400
14.	Newport Beach Pier	1,322
15.	Harford Pier	1,320
16.	Pacifica Pier	1,320
17.	Venice Pier	1,310
18.	San Clemente Pier	1,296
19.	Pismo Beach Pier	1,250
20.	Scripps Pier	1,090
21.	Santa Monica Pier	1,080
22.	Hermosa Beach Pier	1,000
23.	Belmont Memorial Pier	975
24.	Cayucos Pier	953
25.	Manhattan Beach Pier	928
26.	Balboa Pier	920
27.	Crescent City Pier	900
28.	Crystal Pie	872
29	Capitola Wharf	855
30.	San Simeon Pier	850
31.	Malibu Pier	780
32.	Fisherman's Wharf, Monterey	750+
33.	Gaviota Pier	529
34.	Trinidad Pier	520
35.	Seacliff State Beach Pier	500
36.	Point Arena Pier	330
37.	Redondo Beach Pier	Horseshoe

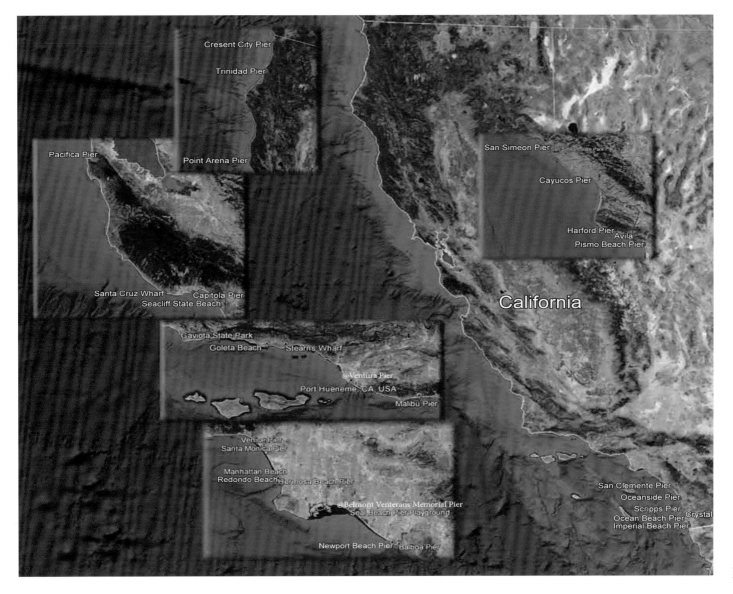

Cresent City Pier

Trinidad Pier

Pacifica Pier

Point Arena Pier

San Simeon Pier

Cayucos Pier

Harford Pier Avila
Pismo Beach Pier

Santa Cruz Wharf Capitola Pier
Seacliff State Beach

California

Gaviota State Park
Goleta Beach Stearns Wharf

@Ventura Pier
Port Hueneme, CA, USA
Malibu Pier

Venice Pier
Santa Monica Pier

Manhattan Beach
Redondo Beach Hermosa Beach Pier

San Clemente Pier
Oceanside Pier
Scripps Pier
Ocean Beach Pier Crystal
Imperial Beach Pier

@Belmont Venterans Memorial Pier
Seal Beach Pier Playground

Newport Beach Pier Balboa Pier

Contributors

Debra Bronow is a writer and consultant to non-profit organizations. Born in California, she grew up near beaches (and sometimes piers) in the South Pacific and Northwestern Alaska, with regular trips back to visit grandparents – and piers – in Southern California. She has been a writer and artist since early childhood. She lives in Southern California, somewhere between the 405 freeway and the beaches of the South Bay, with her husband, two sons, and a standard poodle. She still believes there is no better treat in the world than a Balboa Bar on a hot summer day.

Serge Dedina is the Executive Director of WILDCOAST, an international conservation team that conserves coastal and marine ecosystems and wildlife. His articles and essays on Imperial Beach have been published in the *San Diego Union-Tribune, Los Angeles Times, Longboard Magazine,* and the *Voice of San Diego.* He is the author of *Saving the Gray Whale, Wild Sea* and the forthcoming *Surfing the Border.* In recognition of his conservation achievements, Serge was awarded the San Diego Zoological Society's Conservation Medal, the California Coastal Commission's Coastal Hero Award and the Surf Industry Manufacturer's Association Environmentalist of the Year Award. Serge grew up in Imperial Beach, worked as an ocean lifeguard there in the 1980s and later as a State of California Lifeguard, and can still be found surfing by the pier when the waves are good.

Christie Forshey has enjoyed residing in beach cities – Torrance, Long Beach, Redondo Beach and Santa Barbara. Christie is an educator and writer who enjoys spending time with her husband Jeff and three children, Theo, Nina and Ruby. Christie earned her Master's Degree at Pepperdine University and completed her undergraduate work in Creative Writing at CSULB. She is a published poet. Christie is great friends with Ed Grant's daughter, Alisha, who met and became roommates in Long Beach and later reunited in Manhattan Beach! The beach has brought us together and kept us together.

John Fry is the President of the Pacific Beach Historical Society. Not quite a native San Diegan, he grew up in what used to be called East San Diego, graduated from San Diego State in 1966 and taught school beginning in 1968. He moved to Pacific Beach in 1970 and, in 1979, he left teaching and co-founded the Pacific Beach Historical Society. He self-published *A Short History of Pacific Beach* and *A Short History of Crystal Pier.* He is also the author of Images of America: Pacific Beach, issued by Arcadia Publishing.

Sam George, former senior editor for Surfing magazine and former editor-in-chief of SURFER magazine has written and/or directed a number of acclaimed surfing documentaries, including *Riding Giants, Pipeline Masters, The Lost Wave: An African Surf Story, Hollywood Don't Surf,* and *The Legend of Eddie Aikau.* Sam has written and edited more than half a dozen books on the subject of surfing, including *Surfing: A Way Of Life, Surfing, Tom Blake: Surfing 1922-1932, The Perfect Day: 40 Years of SURFER Magazine, Surf Life. SURFER 50,* and *The Big Juice.* A former professional competitor Sam was also one of the pioneers of stand-up paddle surfing and is currently the Senior Editor of *SUP Magazine*. He still competes in various stand-up paddle surf races, accruing a number

John Hinkle born in Dallas Tx, raised in Houston, a graduate of Stephen F. Austin State University, BA communications, Journalism, 1979. First worked as sports writer for the Baytown Sun, Baytown Texas and spent time surfing nearby Galveston. Moved to the hill country of Austin Texas working as a copy editor for the Austin American Statesman before finally relocating to Los Angeles in 1982 working for the *Los Angeles Herald Examiner*. A career shift in 1984, joining IATSE Local 729, Hinkle has worked the last 30 years as a scenic artist for motion pictures and television and became a member of the MALIBU SURFING ASSOCIATION in 2005 serving as MSA President since 2012. He has two sons, Austin and Jesse, who grew up surfing the waves of First Point, Malibu.

Cathy and Don Inglesias have lived close to the beach in Santa Cruz since the late 1970s. Don has been surfing for over 50 years and still loves the power and rhythm of the waves. Cathy and Don, along with a core group of Santa Cruz surf families, began the Santa Cruz Woodies Car Club in 1993, at a collective gathering, in their living room. The car club is still going strong after 20 years. They share their passion for old cars and the beach lifestyle and hope to do so for another 50 years.

Iris King was born and raised in Santa Barbara County. She joined the United States Marine Corps Reserves when she was 17 and served for 8 years. During that time she attended UCSB and became a California State Lifeguard. In 2007 she was offered a permanent Peace Officer position with State Parks and currently works as a Permanent Lifeguard along the Gaviota Coast. In her spare time she enjoys surfing, fishing, diving and gardening.

Larry Krueger is an instructor of Communication Studies courses for over 25 years at local Southern California colleges and universities and has won numerous academic awards. He lived in Seal Beach for over 30 years and now lives in Belmont Shore. He is a waterman who loves to surf, fish, and spearfish Baja and the local waters. Most importantly, he is a husband and father teaching his children to love the sea, learning, and life.

Steve Long is a retired State Park Lifeguard Chief who oversaw lifeguard services at Doheny, San Clemente and San Onofre State Beaches for 30 years. A life long surfer, he began frequenting the beaches in San Clemente in 1961, raising a family there from 1978 to the present. An armchair historian, he volunteers his time presenting stories and preparing exhibits for the San Onofre Parks Foundation in San Clemente.

Marikay Grant Lindstrom is the big sister to author Ed Grant. They have a baby sister, Anita Elliott who lives in Oregon. The two older siblings frequently told Anita she was adopted just to see her cry. Their father Andrew Grant was a WWII aviator, Marikay, the only one in the family to get flying genes, lives in Santa Paula, California, very near the Santa Paula Airport, owns two small aircraft a pink Piper Cherokee and a Citabria. Each week she and husband Bill along with precocious little dog Lily fly to a second home in Big Bear, California. It was at the high altitude Big Bear Airport she flew Charter and was the airport Chief pilot. She is a member of the Ninety-Nines, International Organization of Women Pilots, an airplane racer and recipient of Professional Pilot of the year for Orange County Chapter.

Randie Marlow is a lifelong resident of coastal California whose photographs have long been favorites of visitors and residents. She is the owner of Images and Digital Design, a full service design and photography business. Images and Digital Design has recently celebrated its 11th year in business. Randie's favorite subjects to shoot range from the wildflowers of Half Moon Bay to breeding bird colonies of the Devil's Slide Trail; from boats moored in the fog at Princeton Harbor to newborn harbor seals and migrating whales at Pigeon Point Lighthouse. She can be reached at itsamarlow@gmail.com.

Frank Quirarte is a photographer extraordinaire and all around waterman. Frank's work has graced the cover and pages of all the finest surfer publications around the world. His list of accomplishments go well beyond the surf industry; from his service in the military to his heroic actions rescuing survivors in New Orleans, Louisiana after Katrina. Frank always puts safety before his photography. He has probably made more rescues at Mavericks than anyone else! His actions have saved countless lives, including Greg Long out at Cortez Bank.

Tracey Thomasson is a graphic designer and art director living in Manhattan Beach, CA. She is passionate about good design and considers herself a typography aficionado. Tracey loves the beach lifestyle and has lived within walking distance of the Redondo, Hermosa and Manhattan Beach piers for her entire life.

Stuart Thornton had the good fortune to experience a lot of the California Coast's finest piers while researching his Moon Coastal California guidebook in 2012. The Marina based writer got better acquainted with the piers while working with the charismatic Ed Grant on this book. In addition to Moon Coastal California, Stuart is the author of *Moon Santa Barbara* and *The Central Coast* and *Moon Spotlight Cambria and San Simeon*. He also contributes to *National Geographic Education,* the *Monterey County Weekly* and *Relix Magazine*.

Mike Wallace has pulled in deep to surf subjects ranging from the origins of the wetsuit to computer-aided surfboard design for various blogs and publications, including *Surfpulse, Good Times, The Inertia* and the *Half Moon Bay Review*. Based in Moss Beach, California, Mike has shaped surfboards for several years under the 'Iconoclast' label in the never-ending search for the optimal combination of retro outlines and modern bottom contours to give more mature surfers a leg up over their younger rivals. He is also the head coach of the Half Moon Bay High Surf Team and has spent several seasons caravanning up and down the California coast in the lee of the state's piers coaching his two groms Konrad and Kaira. This has informed his unique perspective on 'Piers of the California Coast' as a window into regional surf culture. By trade he is a market strategist for *Action Economics* and has been posted in Washington, London and Bay Area covering the international financial markets for the past two decades.

Grant Washburn, world-class big wave surfer, was featured in the Imax film *Adventures in Wild California*, and the award winning surf documentary, *Riding Giants*. He was the Surf Coordinator on *Chasing Mavericks*, the story of iconic big wave surfer Jay Moriarty. Washburn co-wrote and edited the large format book *Inside Maverick's, Portrait of a Monster Wave*. Washburn is currently competing in the Big Wave World Tour as well as doing the color commentary.